SAVANNAH IN HISTORY

A GUIDE TO MORE THAN 75 SITES IN HISTORICAL CONTEXT

RODNEY AND LORETTA CARLISLE

Globe
Pequot

Guilford, Connecticut

Globe
Pequot

An imprint of The Rowman & Littlefield Publishing Group, Inc.
4501 Forbes Blvd., Ste. 200
Lanham, MD 20706
www.rowman.com

Distributed by NATIONAL BOOK NETWORK

British Library Cataloguing in Publication Information available

Library of Congress Cataloging-in-Publication Data available
Names: Carlisle, Rodney P., author. | Carlisle, Loretta, author.
Title: Savannah in history : a guide to more than 75 sites in historical context / Rodney Carlisle and Loretta Carlisle.
Description: Guilford, Connecticut : Globe Pequot, an imprint of the Rowman & Littlefield Publishing Group, 2019. | Includes index.
Identifiers: LCCN 2018051084 (print) | LCCN 2018052556 (ebook) | ISBN 9781683340287 (electronic) | ISBN 9781683340270 (pbk. : alk. paper)
Subjects: LCSH: Historic sites—Georgia—Savannah—Guidebooks. | Savannah (Ga.)—History—Guidebooks. | Savannah (Ga.)—Tours.
Classification: LCC F294.S2 (ebook) | LCC F294.S2 C37 2019 (print) | DDC 917.58/72404—dc23
LC record available at https://lccn.loc.gov/2018051084

♾™ The paper used in this publication meets the minimum requirements of American National Standard for Information Sciences—Permanence of Paper for Printed Library Materials, ANSI/NISO Z39.48-1992

Printed in the United States of America

Contents

Acknowledgments

During our research and photography tours of Savannah, many individuals provided kind advice and information. Among those who helped answer questions were Aaron Bradford and Justin Childers at Old Fort Jackson. Bill Saunders hosted us around the Railroad Museum on a bitter cold day, providing fascinating details of railroad history. Gary Webb gave us a personal tour of the Webb Museum and supplied all sorts of information on many of the exhibits. Sculptor Susie Chisholm answered several of our questions about her statue of Johnny Mercer. Dave Folley, our research assistant, investigated and evaluated a host of internet websites.

In addition, many gracious citizens of Savannah assisted with driving and parking directions, information, and suggestions.

We thank them all.

—Rodney and Loretta Carlisle

Introduction

Savannah is one of the most historically interesting cities in the United States. Most of the city's more than two dozen squares and parks contain at least one statue, monument, or preserved historical object. Each commemorates an event, a person, an ethnic group, or a legend that evokes a specific moment or period in history. Whole blocks of homes and other buildings, such as inns, restaurants, and churches, many built much more than a century ago and carefully preserved or restored, add to the city's flavor of the past, as do collections of artifacts in the city's museums.

However, for visitors and many longtime residents of Savannah, the sheer number of places, buildings, monuments, and collections can create a blurred set of impressions of the past. Walking or auto tours, with or without a guide, can be almost overwhelming. Sites are usually seen in random order as encountered along street routes and in neighborhoods, rather than in time sequence.

This guidebook presents more than seventy-five sites grouped in *chronological* (that is, historical) order, rather than in a street-by-street sequence. Seen this way, the monuments, buildings, and major artifacts document history in a tangible way. The physical items you can see tell the story of the city's history and its place in the history of Georgia, the United States, and the world.

When history is told through places, buildings, monuments, and artifacts, rather than through papers such as letters, journals, and official government documents, it brings to life specific facts of the story. A tangible item you can see firsthand often speaks more loudly than a printed account.

Savannah, the first town established by English settlers in Georgia, reflected several ideas that were very advanced for the late 1700s: city planning, prohibition of slavery, and banning of alcohol. Of course, slavery and alcohol soon came to the colony. Yet the thoughtful city plan survives to the present in the striking form of street layout and many small park-like squares and in the locations of churches and civic buildings.

Events and decisions of later eras, most repeatedly told in textbooks and classrooms, also come alive in tangible ways. In the Civil War, after Union general William T. Sherman's troops left Atlanta burning behind them and marched across Georgia, leaving a swath of destruction, Sherman unexpectedly spared Savannah from a similar fate. The headquarters house where he notified Lincoln that he had spared the city still stands, and the result of his decision is visible when present-day visitors look at the same homes and churches he decided to preserve from the destruction of war and revenge.

The city had its share of unique characters, some famous in the region or nationally, and others more obscure, including men and women, white, black, and Native American. Dozens of these people are remembered with monuments and, sometimes, the houses that they lived in and the very things they handled. These places evoke the stories of artists, writers, clergymen, musicians, performers, jurists, entrepreneurs, military officers, and political leaders. Heroes and villains (and some ghosts) all have stories associated with specific buildings, artifacts, and spots in the city that Sherman left undestroyed.

This guidebook groups the places to see into seven periods:

- First Settlement and Colonial Era: 1733–1774
- American Revolution and Early National Period: 1775–1815
- Antebellum Period: 1816–1860
- Civil War and Reconstruction: 1861–1876
- Age of Enterprise through World War I: 1877–1918
- Mid-twentieth Century: 1919–1979
- Modern Savannah: 1980 to the Present

For visitors and residents, the sites, monuments, and objects are three-dimensional documents that back up and tell the stories. This guide provides you with a tool to read the history of Savannah, the South, and the United States, laid out in this physical way.

Please note that all phone numbers mentioned in this book are current as the book goes to press but, of course, are subject to change and may need to be rechecked from current sources.

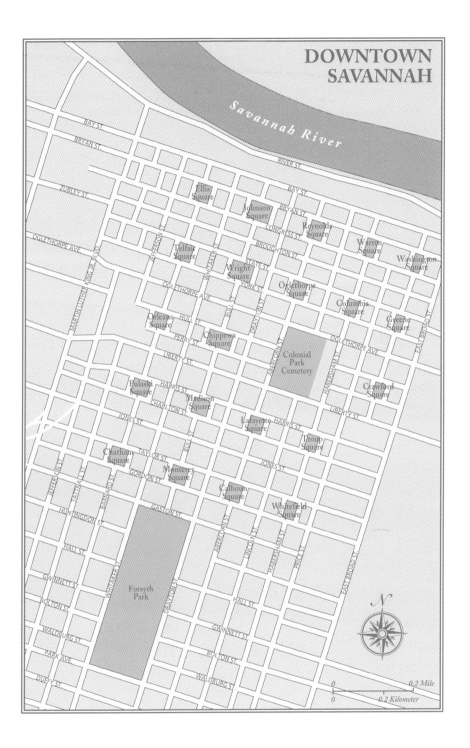

DOWNTOWN SAVANNAH

Savannah River

BAY ST.

BRYAN ST.

RIVER ST.

ZUBLEY ST.

BAY ST.

Ellis Square

BRYAN ST.

Johnson Square

CONGRESS ST.

Reynolds Square

OGLETHORPE AVE.

BROUGHTON ST.

Telfair Square

STATE ST.

Warren Square

Washington Square

MARTIN LUTHER KING JR. BLVD.

JEFFERSON ST.

WHITAKER ST.

Wright Square

YORK ST.

Oglethorpe Square

DRAYTON ST.

OGLETHORPE AVE.

Columbia Square

Orleans Square

HULL ST.

Greene Square

EAST BROAD ST.

Chippewa Square

PERRY ST.

Colonial Park Cemetery

OGLETHORPE AVE.

LIBERTY ST.

ABERCORN ST.

HABERSHAM ST.

Pulaski Square

HARRIS ST.

Crawford Square

Madison Square

CHARLTON ST.

LIBERTY ST.

JONES ST.

Lafayette Square

HARRIS ST.

HULL ST.

Troup Square

Chatham Square

TAYLOR ST.

Monterey Square

GORDON ST.

JONES ST.

JEFFERSON ST.

TATTNALL ST.

BARNARD ST.

Calhoun Square

Whitefield Square

HUNTINGDON ST.

GASTON ST.

ABERCORN ST.

LINCOLN ST.

HABERSHAM ST.

PRICE ST.

EAST BROAD ST.

HALL ST.

GWINNETT ST.

WHITAKER ST.

Forsyth Park

DRAYTON ST.

BOLTON ST.

HALL ST.

WALDBURG ST.

GWINNETT ST.

PARK AVE.

BOLTON ST.

DUFFY ST.

WALDBURG ST.

N

0   0.2 Mile

0   0.2 Kilometer

1 First Settlement and Colonial Era, 1733–1774

The colony of Georgia was unique in several ways among the thirteen colonies that later declared their independence from Britain to form the United States of America. It was the last colony to be founded, in 1733, more than a century after the founding of Jamestown (1607), Plymouth (1620), and Massachusetts (1630). The British government at first regarded the colony of Georgia as a military outpost, to guard the other colonies against Spanish incursions from Florida, a territory held by the Spanish since 1565. During 1739–1748, the local version of the War of Austrian Succession (a British-Spanish war), known locally as "The War of Jenkins' Ear," included invasions by several units of British troops from Georgia into northern Florida, with two attacks on the Spanish fort at St. Augustine. Under James Oglethorpe, the local British forces held off a final Spanish counterattack into Georgia at the Battle of Bloody Marsh on St. Simons Island, July 1742. St. Simons Island is about seventy miles south of Savannah and about forty miles north of the Florida-Georgia border.

The founders of Georgia had idealistic plans to have the colony serve not only as a military buffer against the Spanish colony of Florida but also as a refuge for impoverished British subjects who would otherwise have been sent to prison for failure to pay debts. The leading founder of the colony, James Oglethorpe, was particularly committed to that cause because a friend of his, Robert Castell, had died of smallpox contracted in Fleet Street Debtor's Prison in London. The founders' idealistic prohibition of slavery and consumption of alcohol in the colony were also unusual goals in the era.

The colony of Georgia, in its first decades from 1733 through 1751, had no official local colony-wide government, instead being ruled remotely from England by the colony's trustees. Oglethorpe himself stayed in the colony for several periods in 1733 and 1739–1743, and, as one of the trustees of the colony and leader of the colonial militia, he was widely regarded as "founder and leader." Even so, he never held the formal position of governor.

Oglethorpe himself was credited with laying out the first town plan for Savannah, which is reflected today in the arrangement of city squares at major intersections. According to the original plan, "trust lots" to the east and west of each square were set aside for public purposes such as churches or courthouses. An experimental garden was established at the east end of the settlement near the river, "Trustees' Garden," to see how various crops would fare in the Georgia climate. The squares themselves were used not simply as parks but also as practice grounds for settlers' militia drills. Each settler family was expected to provide one able-bodied adult male for the militia. The concept of city and social planning was much discussed in Europe by utopian writers and others, but very few cities anywhere in the world in the 1700s actually carried through on an urban plan as well as Savannah.

Oglethorpe and the first settlers were very lucky to encounter an unusual Native American settlement at the Yamacraw town site where they built Savannah. Led by Tomochichi, Yamacraw Village had members of both the Creek and the Yamasee tribes, who were frequently at war with each other in this period. Tomochichi had established the town in an effort to bring peace to the region and the two Native American peoples. When the British settlers arrived, Tomochichi granted his own town territory (which reached from the Savannah River south to present-day Liberty Street) to the British settlers. He helpfully made way for the British by moving his own settlement slightly to the west, to a section known as Yamacraw Village. That name survives now to describe a housing development and neighborhood along the western side of downtown Savannah.

Oglethorpe was also fortunate in encountering a woman, Mary Musgrove, the daughter of an English officer and a Native American princess, who served as a translator and mediator. She was also a very competent businesswoman, operating trading posts and acquiring rights to real estate from both English and Native American governments.

Oglethorpe and the other trustees had high hopes that the colony would provide a good climate for raising silkworms, and they experimented with planting mulberry trees, on which silkworms grow and feed. Through the colonial period (the 1600s and 1700s), both the British government and British entrepreneurs hoped to develop silk production in

Mary Musgrove

Mary Musgrove Bosomworth was born of mixed Creek and English ancestry in 1700 in a small Creek settlement on the Ocmulgee River, now located in Georgia. Her father was an English trader, Edward Griffin, and her mother was a Creek princess. Because of customs of the Creeks that traced ancestry through the maternal side, they regarded her as a member of their tribe. From about 1710 to 1715, Mary lived with her English father's family in South Carolina, where she was educated and brought up as a Christian.

Because she was fluent in both English and the Creek language, Mary was a valuable diplomat and translator, working with Oglethorpe in negotiations with Tomochichi and other Native American leaders.

She had three marriages, outliving her first two husbands. Her third husband was a prominent English clergyman, Thomas Bosomworth. The Creek tribe deeded three large Sea Islands to the couple: Sapelo, Ossabaw, and St. Catherines. The English at first rejected the Bosomworth claims to the land on the grounds that nations, such as the Creek, could not grant lands to individuals—only to other nations. However, in 1758, the British settled the dispute by granting to Mary and her husband St. Catherines Island, as well as the cash from the sale of Sapelo and Ossabaw Islands. When Mary died in 1765, Bosomworth inherited all of her property; in later years, it passed on to his descendants.

Today, one of the "Savannah Belles Ferries" that runs between the Savannah waterfront to the Convention Center bears Mary Musgrove's name.

Deerskin trader. This display in the Savannah History Museum represents one of the most successful enterprises of the colonial period, the trade in deerskins exported to Europe for use in gloves and other fine leatherwork goods.

several American colonies, as the cloth was expensive and in high demand. Virtually all silk in Britain was imported from the Far East, France, or Italy. For that reason, colonists in Virginia, the Carolinas, and Georgia all experimented (with very little success) in raising mulberry trees, importing silkworms, and attempting to develop a silk trade.

In the colonial period, fortunes could be made in such products as deer hides (in wide demand in Europe for the manufacture of fine leather goods such as gloves) and turpentine and pitch from the abundant pine forests. Through the coastal and interior regions of Georgia, numerous trading posts were set up by enterprising individuals who exchanged cheap European goods for the valuable deerskins and forest products.

Georgia colonists also hoped to emulate their neighbors in South Carolina with the production and export of cotton, rice, or indigo. Indigo—the source of an excellent blue dye—had a brief success in both colonies since Britain protected the crop by prohibiting importation of indigo from non-British colonies, but after the American War of Independence, without the protected market, indigo plantations closed down or converted to other crops.

By the 1740s, white settlers in Georgia had complained of the restriction prohibiting slavery, and settlers both from Great Britain and coming by land from South Carolina began violating the antislavery restriction, bringing in slaves from South Carolina or buying them from dealers who brought them by sea from other British colonies, from Cuba, or even directly from Africa. The prohibition on slavery in Georgia was formally lifted in 1751 in the face of the settlers' demands.

Like the prohibition on slavery, the idealistic ban on alcoholic beverages was almost impossible to enforce, and it, too, was abandoned. In 1751, the British government replaced the earlier system of governance by a remote group of trustees with a locally elected legislature and a governor appointed by the British Crown, a royal colony system identical to that in South Carolina.

By the mid-1750s, Georgia resembled other British colonies in many respects. Besides taverns, liquor, and slaves, large plantations flourished. The plantations were owned and operated by a growing class of "planters"—wealthy landowners committed to preserving and expanding the plantation system. The term was a bit misleading, as most planters never actually "planted" any crops themselves, instead relying on slaves or indentured servants to do the actual work. Savannah not only included town homes of planters but also hosted numerous businesses that thrived on shipping the plantation products out and importing luxury goods, furnishings, and manufactured products for local consumption.

On the flats above the bluffs, the small and growing town took shape around the public squares, and a proliferation of churches representing several different denominations took advantage of the colony's renowned tolerance for religious variation. Those included not only the Anglican/Episcopal Church (1733) and a Masonic lodge (founded by Oglethorpe himself in 1733/1734) but also a Jewish congregation, Mickve Israel (1735), and a Lutheran church (1741).

Today, throughout Savannah, there are dozens of physical remnants of this colonial era. They include the town shape itself, monuments, and several buildings. Although the physical churches built in the colonial period were later lost to fires and storms, some present-day congregations trace their origins to Savannah's first years. Some of the most accessible of the sites that represent the colonial era are described below.

SITES

OGLETHORPE MEMORIALS

The city of Savannah, its location, and its regular, handsome layout of streets with parks at intersections *all* serve as memorials to the founder of the city and of Georgia, James Oglethorpe. However, in 1906, the Georgia branch of the Colonial Dames of America established a small specific Oglethorpe monument, a marble bench, which is now in a little park area in front of the Hyatt Hotel near the corner of West Bay and Whitaker Streets. A nearby historical marker about one hundred feet to the east of the bench provides details. The marker, titled "Landing of Oglethorpe and the Colonists," gives the route and dates of Oglethorpe's first expedition and settlement on the site.

While it is impossible to know whether the spot of the bench is *precisely* where Oglethorpe "pitched his tent," it is probably quite close to the exact location.

In 1910, four years after the bench was installed, a committee erected a more imposing monument, a nine-foot bronze statue of Oglethorpe as general, located in Chippewa Square, at the intersection of Bull Street and Hull Street. As noted on the statue's plaque, funds were provided not only by patriotic societies but also by the State of

Oglethorpe Bench. This marble bench on Bay Street marks the spot where Oglethorpe and the first colonists from Britain climbed the bluff and pitched their tents to found Savannah and the colony of Georgia.

Oglethorpe Monument. Shown in this statue in his military uniform, George Oglethorpe faces south in Chippewa Square, as if defending the colony of Georgia from possible Spanish attack from Florida.

Georgia and the City of Savannah. The statue faces south, according to legend, "so he can keep an eye on the Spanish." The statue was designed by Daniel Chester French, who also designed the seated statue of Lincoln in the Lincoln Memorial in Washington, D.C., among other major monuments and statues.

TOMOCHICHI ROCK, WRIGHT SQUARE

Tomochichi, the chief of the Yamacraw, the Native American people encountered by Oglethorpe and the first English settlers in Savannah, developed a close relationship with Oglethorpe. The Yamacraw were a group of about two hundred Creek and Yamasee Indians, organized by Tomochichi himself, who had settled in the very spot that Oglethorpe chose for his first settlement at Savannah. By agreeing to resettle his people, Tomochichi avoided the conflicts that had characterized

many other first European settlements in the other twelve colonies to the north.

In some accounts, Tomochichi's friendly reception of the colonists entitles him to be regarded as "cofounder" of the colony of Georgia. At Oglethorpe's invitation, Tomochichi and his wife visited Britain in 1735, where he met with King George II and the archbishop of Canterbury.

Tomochichi died in 1739, and his remains were buried in Wright Square at the intersection of Bull and York Streets. A pyramid of stones was erected over his grave and served as a marker for more than 140 years. However, the pyramid was removed to make space for a monument erected in 1883, to William Washington Gordon, the founder of the Central of Georgia Railroad. The Gordon Monument in the center of Wright Square was funded by the railroad company.

Tomochichi Rock. The body of the Native American chief Tomochichi was moved from the center of Wright Square to the southeast corner of the square and marked with a massive boulder.

Gordon's daughter-in-law, Nellie Kinzie Gordon (the mother of Juliette Gordon Low, founder of the Girl Scouts, discussed in a later chapter), worked with others in the Colonial Dames of Georgia organization to erect a new memorial to Tomochichi. That organization funded the present memorial to Tomochichi in the form of a large boulder of granite brought from Stone Mountain, Georgia, and installed April 21, 1899. The stone monument is known locally as "Tomochichi Rock" or "Tomochichi's Grave Rock." It is located at the southeast corner of the tree-shaded square where the north-bound lane of Bull Street curves around the square. The stone has an inset plaque and is accompanied by a historical marker erected in 1952, which together give additional details of the life of Tomochichi.

TRUSTEES' GARDEN AND "FORT WAYNE"

An experimental garden, to try out various crops in the Georgia climate, was located at East Bay and East Broad Streets. Today, the locale hosts the Charles Morris Center (a venue for weddings and other events), the nearby Pirates' House Restaurant, and, slightly to the east, the location of Fort Wayne. The sign for Trustees' Garden on East Bay now graces a parking lot. All vestiges of the garden itself have long ago vanished.

A buttressed wall, a block to the east, often thought to be part of the remains of Fort Wayne, is actually a more recent brick con-struction for the Savannah Waterworks, built in 1853. Fort Wayne itself was a name given in later years to a fort that protected the city from attack by ships coming up the Savannah River (discussed in the next chapter).

PIRATES' HOUSE AND HERB HOUSE

20 East Broad Street
(912) 233-5757

Closely associated (and right next door) to the former site of the Trustees' Garden is the Pirates' House Restaurant. Incorporated in the East Broad Street side of the building is the older Herb House, reputedly built in 1734 and considered the oldest building still standing in Savannah. The Herb House itself was originally used to house the gardener for the Trustees' Garden. The gardener's office and tool storage were in the front of the building, with a stable in the back and a hayloft above. The Herb House was constructed from bricks manufactured a block away, below the bluff facing the Savannah River, where the first colonists had set up a brickworks the year before.

By the early 1750s, the Trustees' Garden was abandoned. Nearby buildings flourished as residences and inns, with the Herb House becoming an inn about that time. With its proximity to the waterfront, the inn soon became a rendezvous for sailors. Today the Pirates' House Restaurant, with its hand-hewn beams, unfaced brick walls, and pirate-themed decor, echoes that early history.

Like several other early Savannah sites, the building has accumulated its share of ghost stories and legends. According to one oft-repeated tale, a tunnel once connected the cellar of the building to the waterfront, through which sailors were shanghaied to work aboard ship. For this and some other haunted locales, check appendix B of this book.

Robert Louis Stevenson tied his fictional character in *Treasure Island*, Captain Flint,

The Pirates' House Restaurant is located in this building, assumed to be the oldest one standing in Savannah. It was originally the location of the residence of the gardener for the "Trustees' Garden."

to Savannah. The children's novel, published in 1883, had Flint dying in Savannah from a rum overdose, presumably at a seaman's tavern very much like the Pirates' House. Flint himself never appeared in the novel, but the book reported legends and accounts by others surrounding him, telling of exploits, his burial of the hidden treasure, and his death from too much rum. Captain Flint (with hints of his Savannah connections) shows up in many adaptations, spin-offs, and movie versions of the Robert Louis Stevenson story.

JOHN WESLEY STATUE AND METHODISM

On Reynolds Square at the intersection of Abercorn Street and East Bryan Street, there is a sculpture of John Wesley, the founder of Methodism. When he lived in Savannah in 1736–1737 as a minister in the Anglican Church, he stayed in the parish house building on the site now occupied by the Planters Inn, which fronts on the square. The bronze statue of Wesley was sculpted by Marshall Harrison Daugherty, both a native of Georgia and a Methodist, and cast in Corona, New York. It was installed on the site in 1969.

Wesley stayed in Savannah only a year and nine months. While in Savannah, he became romantically involved with a young woman, Sophia Hopkey, but when she married another man, Wesley denied her access to communion, earning him the enmity of her family and others. He also got in trouble with local church-goers for refusing to adopt the local practice of baptism by sprinkling, insisting that baptism be conducted by immersion in water. Although this dispute was a matter of church policy, Thomas Causton, Sophia's uncle, brought criminal charges against Wesley that included

John Wesley Statue. Although John Wesley stayed in the Georgia colony for less than two years, he angered the colonial parishioners and departed under intense criticism. After returning to Britain, he earned fame as the founder of Methodism.

Reynolds Square Colonial Sites

While all of the squares in Savannah have buildings and monuments from different periods, Reynolds Square, where Abercorn Street meets East Congress Street, has several reminders of the colonial period. In the center of the square is the statue of John Wesley, who lived in colonial Savannah from 1736 to 1737. The Planters Inn at 29 Abercorn is actually on the spot of the parsonage in which Wesley stayed.

A building once stood at the corner of Bryan and Abercorn, on the north side of the square, known as the "Old Filature House." Built in 1751, it was intended to house the silk-weaving business, which, of course, never succeeded in Savannah or elsewhere in the colonies. Its high point may have been 1764, when silk weavers from the nearby town of Ebenezer processed some fifteen thousand pounds of silk at the Filature.

When George Washington toured Savannah in 1791, a lavish dinner and reception for the president was held in the building. The Filature House burned down before 1850; a historical marker at East St. Julian Street between Lincoln and Abercorn on the east side of the square marks the site of the structure.

refusing to baptize infants in the local manner. Realizing he was no longer welcome in the colony, Wesley took passage to Charleston, and thence back to England.

Two years after his return to England, he began his own ministry, preaching against the notion of predestination—that is, that salvation of individuals was predestined. Instead, he argued, one could achieve salvation by leading a Christian life. This doctrine came to be known as "Methodism," although Wesley remained within the Anglican Church as he continued to preach his message. After the American Revolution, Wesley began to ordain ministers to serve in the United States. A separate Methodist church was established in Baltimore in 1784, and this date is often taken as the formal birth of Methodism.

WORMSLOE STATE HISTORIC SITE

7601 Skidaway Road
(912) 353-3023

Reached by way of the Harry S. Truman Parkway and Skidaway Road, Wormsloe is a state-operated historic plantation about nine miles from downtown Savannah. The plantation was established by Noble Jones, a carpenter who came to Georgia in 1733 with Oglethorpe. He built the original plantation home, constructed of tabby (an early form of concrete, using oyster shells), the ruins of which still survive. The ruins are regarded as the oldest remnant of a colonial structure in the Savannah region, predating any building in the city of Savannah itself.

In the first years of the colony, when slavery was prohibited, Noble Jones at first used indentured servants to work the plantation. With the removal of the prohibition on slavery in 1751, Jones bought slaves, and they planted various crops, including rice, corn, fruits, and vegetables. Like others, he experimented with mulberry trees and the raising of silkworms. Although his crops never paid off, Jones continued to acquire town and country real estate, and he served as judge, legislator, and surveyor, as well as militia captain. As a surveyor, he was responsible for laying out two towns: Augusta and New Ebenezer; as militia officer, he had commanded a company of marines who defended Georgia against the Spanish during the War of Jenkins' Ear (1739–1748). He died at the beginning of the American Revolution. Although Noble Jones was a

Wormsloe Plantation Drive. Like many other grand plantations of the colonial and early national period, Wormsloe is entered by way of an oak-shadowed lane. The drive leads back to a visitors' center and, beyond it, to the ruins of the original plantation.

Loyalist, his son, Noble Wimberly Jones, was an ardent Patriot.

Probably because of the political differences with his son, Noble Jones willed the estate to his daughter, Mary Jones Bulloch. But Noble Jones stipulated that on her death, the estate should pass to Noble Wimberly Jones and to his heirs "forever." In 1828, Noble Wimberly Jones's son, George Jones, built the elaborate plantation home that still stands. Through the antebellum decades, the plantation was engaged in cotton production, like many of the other large Savannah-area plantations.

Doctor Noble Wimberly Jones

The son of Noble Jones, the planter who established Wormsloe, was a prominent Patriot in the American Revolution, despite the fact that his father was a Loyalist. The younger Jones, who came to the colony with his father in 1733, was a doctor. He was elected Speaker of the Commons House of the colony in 1768. He worked to get Benjamin Franklin to serve as Georgia's agent in London, to carry the complaints of Georgia to Parliament.

Georgia's colonial governor, James Wright, regarded the younger Noble Jones as a threat, and whenever the colonial legislature elected Jones as Speaker, the governor would dissolve the legislature. In defiance, the legislature continually reelected Jones over and over in the years 1771–1773. During the Revolution, Doctor Jones was captured and held prisoner, first in Charleston, then in Florida. After the war, Dr. Noble Wimberly Jones helped set up the visit of George Washington to Savannah in 1791 and, as a doctor, was one of the founders of the Georgia Medical Society in 1804.

Wormsloe Plantation ruins show both brick and tabby construction. The house had fortress-like thick walls.

Wormsloe Plantation sign. Over the entrance to Wormsloe, the sign on the gate documents the date of first settlement and the erection of the entrance arch 180 years later.

The estate remained in the Jones family until 1973, when they deeded it to the state to be operated as a historic site, with the exception of eighty acres and the 1828 plantation home. Today eighth-generation descendants of the original Jones family retain that property. Visitors can see the tabby ruins of the original fortress-like plantation home and inspect artifacts from the colonial era that have been found on the plantation ground in a museum. Costumed interpreters demonstrate crafts of the colonial period. Call ahead for scheduled special events such as a "Colonial Faire and Muster."

TEMPLE MICKVE ISRAEL (ORGANIZED 1735)

The imposing Gothic building, Congregation Mickve Israel, at 20 East Gordon Street, was built in 1876.

Congregation Mickve Israel is the oldest Jewish congregation in Georgia, rivaling the Kahal Kadosh Beth Elohim Congregation in Charleston for the title of the oldest in the South. Charleston's congregation was organized in 1749; Savannah's was set up fourteen years earlier, in 1735. Both congregations demonstrate that Jewish settlement and religious practices were officially accepted and "tolerated" in the southern colonies decades before the American Revolution.

The Savannah congregation traces its ancestry to a group that arrived in July 1733, aboard the ship *William and Sarah*. The original group of forty-two included thirty-four Sephardic Jews—that is, Jews from Spain and Portugal who had lived through the Inquisition there by secretly practicing Judaism while pretending to be Catholic. The other eighteen in the group were Ashkenazic Jews, descended from Jews in Germany. These first

Temple Mickve Israel traces its origins back to the first congregation of the Jewish faith in the colony of Georgia, rivaling a Jewish temple in Charleston for the place of oldest in the South.

Jewish immigrants to Savannah brought with them a Torah scroll, still preserved at Mickve Israel, thought to originate from the Sephardic group because of its material and style.

The charter of the congregation was granted in 1790 by the state of Georgia's first governor, Edward Telfair. The congregation went through several buildings, the first one built in 1820, burning down in 1829. Another, built of brick in 1841, was outgrown by 1870. Construction on the present large Gothic-style synagogue began in 1876 and was completed in 1878. Meanwhile, the congregation had shifted its focus to Reform Judaism. Today, the building is open for tours where docents describe the Gothic sanctuary, museum holdings, and the original stained-glass windows. Although the building is itself representative of the late nineteenth century, the congregation can rightly claim that its organization dates back to the earliest years of the Georgia colony.

THE PINK HOUSE

The Olde Pink House Restaurant and Piano Bar is found on Reynolds Square, at the corner of East Bryan Street. The building dates to the end of the colonial period just before the American Revolution. It was built in 1771 for James Habersham Jr., a cotton factor, who was later a devoted Loyalist during the Revolution. His sons, however, joined the Patriot cause.

The house survived a major city fire in 1796 and passed through ownership of several families. Through the whole antebellum period and the Civil War, to 1865, it housed the Planters Bank and the First Bank of Georgia.

The Pink House is a classic Federal-style building, with a handsome Palladian window over the portico at the front entrance. The pink color, according to legend, stems from the fact that the original red-brick color bled through the coatings of white paint repeatedly applied, until finally, in a 1920s restoration, the then owner decided to accept the color and had the structure painted pink. Today the house hosts a fine dining restaurant, with a tavern in the basement.

Pink House Restaurant.

Whitefield Chapel, Bethesda Academy. The Bethesda Academy, a school for boys, was established by George Whitefield in 1740. The chapel and other buildings at the academy capture the colonial style.

The Pink House is prominently listed in all accounts of Savannah ghosts, with stories of different apparitions both in the upstairs rooms and in the basement tavern.

BETHESDA ACADEMY

9520 Ferguson Avenue, situated about twelve miles south of downtown Savannah, via the Truman Parkway and Whitefield Avenue Museum on-site: (912) 401-0663

A surviving institution from the colonial period is the Bethesda Academy, originally known as the Bethesda Home for Boys. The name "Bethesda" is derived from *beth hesda* (Aramaic words meaning "house of mercy").

An on-site museum presents artifacts and informative panels describing the institution's history.

Founded by the Methodist preacher and philanthropist George Whitefield in 1740, the institution was planned as a trade school for orphan boys, with the hope that it would evolve into a college. As a traveling evangelist, Whitefield raised funds for the Home for Boys through the colonies. Despite a suggestion from Benjamin Franklin that the school might receive more financial support if it moved to Philadelphia, Whitefield insisted it remain in Georgia.

Whitefield died in 1770, but the school continued in operation. After destructive fires in 1773 and 1805, the school was rebuilt on the site in the late 1850s. The school has offered education and a residential setting for boys ever since. Today the facility is both a boarding and a day school.

TYBEE ISLAND LIGHTHOUSE

30 Meddin Drive, Tybee Island, GA 31328
(912) 786-5801

Tybee Island is about eighteen miles east of Savannah by way of U.S. Highway 80. Call ahead for hours of operation, fees, and tour information.

The site of the Tybee Island Lighthouse dates back to the earliest colonial period in Georgia. A wooden tower at the spot was placed at the orders of James Oglethorpe in 1736.

After a storm in 1741, a stone replacement tower was built. The stone tower, without a light, was undermined by shore erosion, and a third tower at the site was built in 1773. That tower was topped by a light and a reflecting lens. After the Civil War, in 1866,

Tybee Island Lighthouse. This lighthouse, one of the oldest on the Atlantic Coast of the United States, is on the same spot chosen for a light by the first colonists.

the 60-foot base of the existing tower was retained and a new tower built on top, to the height of 154 feet.

Further modifications, repairs, and improvements have been made over the decades, all detailed in the lighthouse museum. After the lighthouse was taken over by the Tybee Island Historical Society, it was repainted in black and white colors that were standard for American lighthouses in the fifty years following 1916.

Although the original wooden tower is no longer there, the fact that a warning tower was built on the site in 1736, and that the base of the current tower dates to 1773, qualifies this lighthouse as one of seven in the continental United States that can trace its origins and at least part of its structure to the colonial period. It is the tallest lighthouse in Georgia.

OTHER MONUMENTS OF INTEREST—FIRST SETTLEMENT AND COLONIAL ERA

From the first settlement of Savannah, the city was notable for involving a wide variety of ethnic groups. Over the centuries, descendants of the various groups put up memorials to these early settlers. In several cases, the monuments were funded by groups with the same ancestry elsewhere in the United States, or even by groups in the country of origin.

MORAVIAN MONUMENT— NORTHEAST CORNER OGLETHORPE SQUARE

The Moravians were members of a Protestant sect, originally from a province in what is now the Czech Republic, who had moved to Saxony in Germany, then came to Savannah in 1735 to set up a mission among the Native Americans. The original mission was at Broughton and Habersham Streets. In 1740, the Moravians left Savannah, later establishing a settlement in Pennsylvania. The monument itself was funded by the Wachovia Historical Society of Winston-Salem, North Carolina.

SALZBURGER MONUMENT—SALZBURGER PARK, BAY STREET BETWEEN LINCOLN AND ABERCORN STREETS

The Salzburgers were from the state of Salzburg in the Austro-Hungarian Empire. Some were among the first to arrive in Savannah in the 1730s and relocated to Ebenezer, Georgia. There they established several mills, a Sunday school, and the first orphanage in the colony. The monument itself was funded in 1994 by the state of Salzburg in Austria.

JEWISH CEMETERY MARKER—MEDIAN OF OGLETHORPE AVENUE AT BULL STREET

As part of the 250th anniversary commem-oration of various ethnic groups in 1983, the trustees of the Mordecai Sheftall Cemetery Trust placed a marker in recognition of the 140 Jewish immigrants who arrived in Savannah on the second immigrant ship to arrive in the colony. As noted on the monument, Oglethorpe himself granted a plot of land for the Jewish cemetery.

ST. ANDREWS MONUMENT—OGLETHORPE AVENUE MEDIAN AT BULL STREET

Another monument at the same intersection, erected in the 250th anniversary period, was an eight-foot, ten-inch granite obelisk erected by the St. Andrews Society to honor immigrants from Scotland who settled in

Savannah. Set up in 1987, the obelisk has iron emblems on it that were obtained from the St. Andrews Cemetery section of Laurel Grove Cemetery.

IRISH MONUMENT—EMMET PARK, EAST BAY AT HABERSHAM STREET

Another ethnic monument put up during the 250th anniversary celebrations in 1983 was a Celtic cross to commemorate Georgians of Irish ancestry, mounted in Emmet Park. The limestone cross was actually hand-carved in County Roscommon in Ireland. The cross is about nine feet high and mounted on a round base that is faced with characteristic Savannah grey brick.

The Celtic cross in Emmet Park, between Bay Street and Factors Walk, honors the many Irish settlers who came to Savannah and Georgia in the colonial and early national periods as well as in later waves of immigration.

THE GERMAN MONUMENT—ORLEANS SQUARE

This five-foot fountain sits in a cast-iron basin, ornamented with leaves and frogs. The monument commemorates German immigrants and was supported by several German ethnic organizations. It was set up in 1989.

SEMI-QUINCENTENNIAL FOUNTAIN—LAFAYETTE SQUARE

The National Society of Colonial Dames in America erected a fountain in Lafayette Square in 1983, 250 years after the foundation of Savannah. The fountain has three tiers, with long-necked waterfowl and four stone frogs that seem set to jump.

THE COLONEL WILLIAM BULL SUNDIAL—JOHNSON SQUARE

Colonel William Bull helped lay out the city plan of Savannah. In 1933, on the two hundredth anniversary of the founding of Savannah, a sundial in Johnson Square was set up in his honor, on a base of granite with four mosaic panels. The sundial was hand-cut by the architect-designer Henrik Wallin.

Sundial. This sundial was put in place in honor of Colonel William Bull, after whom Bull Street was named and who conceived the street plan of Savannah.

COLONIAL ROAD MARKERS AND CANNON—MADISON SQUARE

In 1920, the Savannah chapter of the Daughters of the American Revolution set up two markers in Madison Square with small cannons mounted on stone pedestals. The markers make note of two colonial roads— the Ogeechee Road (considered the first road laid out in Georgia) and the Augusta Road, both thought to originate from points nearby. Ogeechee Road, now part of Georgia Route 17, headed southwest from Savannah toward the Ogeechee River, while Augusta Road, now part of Georgia Route 21, headed northwest toward Augusta, Georgia.

Madison Square Cannon. This cannon and marker documents the point of origin of the "Ogeechee Road," presumed to be the first road laid out in Georgia early in the colonial period.

2 American Revolution and Early National Period, 1775–1815

The United States fought the American Revolution (or War of Independence) over the years 1775–1783; three decades years later, the United States fought a "Second War of Independence," the War of 1812, against Britain. The American Revolution and the War of 1812 both impacted Savannah, and forts built during the two wars became local landmarks.

In the Revolution, the British held Savannah after defeating Patriot forces there in December 1778 until evacuating the city on July 11, 1782. Patriot troops, aided by a contingent of French colonial troops, including many black troops from Saint-Domingue (the French colony and later the independent nation of Haiti), fought unsuccessfully in the "Second Battle of Savannah" to liberate the city from British control in October 1779. The site of this battle is well documented with a modern outdoor redoubt reproduction and display.

With the momentous events of both war periods—the Revolution and the War of 1812—Savannah citizens continued the practice of memorializing battles, local and national military leaders and heroes, and national political figures with the naming and renaming of squares and emplacing monuments and statues at spots around the city, many of which survive to the present. Among the heroes of the Revolution remembered in Savannah were the Polish officer Casimir Pulaski, who was killed while leading a force against the British occupiers of Savannah in the unsuccessful battle of 1779, and Rhode Island–born General Nathanael Greene, who successfully liberated much of the interior of Georgia from British control. In recent years, a monument to the Haitians who participated in

the Patriot attempt to liberate Savannah from the British was also erected in Savannah.

In 1791, the first president of the United States, George Washington, toured the states. His tour was both a means of learning local opinion and a gesture to unify the new nation. In May, he visited Georgia. On May 12, he made a stop at Purrysburg on the South Carolina side of the Savannah River (a small town near Hardeeville is still at the site). Georgia officials met Washington there and then accompanied him on a barge trip downriver to Savannah. On the way, the party stopped at Mulberry Grove Plantation, the home of Catherine Greene, the widow of General Nathanael Greene. Washington then went on to Savannah for four days of receptions and dinners, one a full-scale ball at the now-vanished Filature Building. He presented a local military unit, the Chatham Artillery, with a gift of two small cannons, which remain carefully preserved.

In Savannah, businesses supporting nearby cotton and rice plantations flourished: including, in Savannah especially, cotton "factors"—that is, businessmen who operated as buyers and sellers of cotton and as intermediaries for cotton planters in dealing with shipping and with purchasers in New England,

Britain, and continental Europe; they also assisted in other business transactions such as real estate and slave buying and selling. The seaport, with its river harbor that could be reached by oceangoing sailing vessels (and, later, by oceangoing steamships), thrived, with warehouses, taverns, inns, ship-equipment shops ("chandlers"), and other businesses.

The War of 1812 between the United States and Great Britain officially lasted from 1812 to 1814, with the famous victory of Andrew Jackson (leading a diverse force of army regulars, militiamen, Native Americans, and free African Americans) over British forces at New Orleans in January 1815. That battle took place after the two countries had already signed a peace treaty, but before word of that settlement arrived. The war had several causes, including the British practice of impressing (drafting) sailors found on American ships at sea who the British believed (or claimed) were British subjects. In addition, the British had made treaties with Native American tribes in the American West, seen as blocking westward settlement.

During the War of 1812, the British attempted to blockade the Georgia coast, but they only succeeded in tying down U.S. forces to protect the area. Meanwhile, the U.S. Army built up some seacoast forts including Fort Morris (or "Fort Defiance"), about forty miles south of Savannah by modern highways.

SITES

BATTLEFIELD MEMORIAL PARK (1779)

At the corner of Martin Luther King Boulevard and Louisville Road on the west side of downtown Savannah is the small Battlefield

Battlefield Sign and Redoubt. After archeological digs, this replica of the redoubt defended by the British against Patriot attack on October 9, 1779, was built to mark a major American defeat in the Revolution.

Memorial Park. The park contains a replica of a redoubt built by the British and defended in the October 9, 1779, Second Battle of Savannah of the American Revolutionary War. The 1779 battle was known as the "Second" Battle of Savannah because Savannah had fallen to the British in the first battle in December 1778, when only light resistance met the British forces who landed by sea.

The site of the Second Battle of Savannah was excavated in the years 2005–2011, and archaeologists uncovered fortifications, debris from the battle, and trenches. During reconstruction of the site, workers erected an embankment to represent the site of the battle. Concrete markers, set flat in the ground just to the west of the earthen fort replica, represent eight hundred fatalities in the battle. Most of the markers are blank, tributes to the dead whose names are lost to history. The troops on the American side included the Second South Carolina Continentals, a French unit, and a cavalry unit under the Polish officer Count Casimir Pulaski. The French unit consisted of a large contingent of more than five hundred black recruits from the island colony of Saint-Domingue.

Although exact figures are not known, the British forces in Savannah at the 1779 battle were in the range of five thousand to seven thousand men. The British had built several redoubts around the city and successfully held off the attack of the combined French, Haitian, and American Patriot troops fighting for the American cause. The British claimed they inflicted more than 1,000 casualties in the October 9, 1779, battle, and the actual count was probably close to that number, with 244 dead, some 600 wounded, and 144 taken prisoners. It was one of the worst defeats of the American Revolution.

PULASKI MONUMENT

In Monterey Square, at the intersection of Bull Street and Taylor Street, there is a tall column topped with a Statue of Liberty, serving as a monument to Count Casimir Pulaski. Pulaski was a Polish cavalry officer who had fought for Polish independence and then, as a refugee, moved to France. There he met Benjamin Franklin, who recommended Pulaski to George Washington. Pulaski served with American forces in the American Revolution and has been credited with saving Washington's life at the Battle of Brandywine on December 11, 1777, near Chadds Ford, Pennsylvania. At his own insistence, Pulaski formed a small unit of horse-mounted troops armed with lances. For this reason, he is regarded as the father of the American cavalry; he is also widely celebrated by Polish Americans as a hero of their heritage.

Washington assigned Pulaski and his cavalry to fight in Georgia, and he participated in the Second Battle of Savannah fought at the site of the Battlefield Memorial Park. Pulaski was fatally wounded by British grapeshot during that battle and died two days later.

The monument itself was erected in 1852 right after Monterey Square was established. According to legend, Pulaski's body was reinterred at the foot of the monument, recently confirmed with scientific evidence.

Along with the support of Europeans like the Marquis de Lafayette, Count Pulaski's service helped demonstrate that the American War for Independence received wide and significant international support.

Pulaski Monument. This monument in Monterey Square marks the actual tomb of Polish cavalry officer Casimir Pulaski, who died from wounds received during the battle of October 9, 1779.

Statue of Lady Liberty on the Pulaski Monument. The Statue of Liberty on the Pulaski Monument is fifty-five feet above the ground, a bit hard to see from below.

NATHANAEL GREENE AND CATHERINE LITTLEFIELD GREENE

Throughout the South there are many memorials to the "Fighting Quaker" from Rhode Island, General Nathanael Greene. They include the town of Greensboro, North Carolina, and Greenville, South Carolina, as well as Greene Square in Savannah. A monument to Greene was erected in Johnson Square, with the cornerstone laid by the Marquis de Lafayette on his tour of the United States in 1825. Greene's body was relocated from Colonial Park Cemetery in 1901 and reburied beneath the monument in Johnson Square.

Greene was the leader credited with liberating most of Georgia from British rule. Despite the Quaker commitment to pacifism, Greene had formed a militia unit in 1774 before the War for Independence began. Greene, along with George Washington, was one of two officers of general rank who served throughout the whole American Revolution.

In the South, despite a series of battlefield losses, Greene's forces continued to gain ground through a war of attrition, driving the British back through 1780 and 1781 to a few port cities, including Charleston and Savannah. The British evacuated Savannah on July 11, 1782. Despite Greene's failure to take the major southern seaports, he was widely hailed as the liberator of much of the South.

After the war, several southern states offered land grants to Greene, as well as to other officers, as rewards for their service. Greene chose to sell estates elsewhere and settled on the grant of Mulberry Grove Plantation about ten miles northwest of Savannah, near the Savannah River. Originally set up as a plantation to raise mulberry trees for possible

Nathanael Greene Monument. The marble obelisk to Nathanael Greene is in Johnson Square. Greene is honored throughout the South as the American general who liberated most of the interior of the southern states from British control during the American Revolution.

silk production, the plantation had been converted to cotton production.

General Greene died in 1786 after a short illness. In 1792, his widow, Catherine Littlefield Greene, invited young Eli Whitney (a fellow New Englander, originally from Massachusetts and a graduate of Yale University in Connecticut) to visit Mulberry Grove; it was there that Whitney invented the cotton gin. His invention

Cotton gin. This modern replica of the cotton gin shows the simple mechanical principle of cleaning cotton.
SMITHSONIAN INSTITUTION

Eli Whitney and the Cotton Gin

Many legends surround Eli Whitney and his invention of the cotton gin while staying at Mulberry Grove at the invitation of Catherine Greene. One is that Mrs. Greene herself suggested the use of brushes to help separate the seeds from the cotton bolls. Some note that Mrs. Greene's plantation manager, Phineas Miller (a fellow Yale graduate with Whitney), may be due more credit for the invention. Miller was certainly the businessman behind the partnership they set up.

It is well known that although Miller and Whitney patented the gin, there were hundreds of the machines made throughout the South without any permission from them, and with no royalties going to their firm. They fought more than sixty unsuccessful lawsuits against the patent infringers. North and South Carolina granted the partners some awards, but Georgia never did so.

would go on to revolutionize cotton production over the next years. The plantation itself has long since disappeared.

HAITIAN MONUMENT, FRANKLIN SQUARE

One of the military units attempting to liberate Savannah from the British on October 9, 1779, was the *Chasseurs-Volontaires de Saint-Domingue*. This regiment consisted of volunteers from the French colony of Saint-Domingue, now the Republic of Haiti. The soldiers of the unit were Afro-Haitians, mostly free men, as well as a few former slaves who secured their freedom by taking up military service. Led by French general Charles Hector, the *comte d'Estaing*, the ten companies of light infantry amounted to 545 men, one of the largest units on the American side in that battle. Although well celebrated in Haiti, the participation of the *Chasseurs-Volontaires de Saint-Domingue* in the American War for Independence has generally received very little notice in the United States. Haitian writers credit the participation of this unit in the American struggle with inspiring leaders in Haiti to fight both for the ending of slavery there and for independence from France.

In 2007–2009, a sculpture by James Mastin documenting the unit's participation in the Savannah battle was set up in Franklin Square, at the intersection of West St. Julian Street and Montgomery Street, at the west end of the City Market.

Among the Haitian troops who served at the Siege of Savannah was Henri Christophe, a young boy at the time. If estimates of his birth date in 1767 are correct, he would have been twelve years old during the Siege of Savannah. For this reason, it was assumed that he may have been a drummer boy (as drummers were often of such an age), and Mastin

Haitian Monument. This monument in Franklin Square honors the troops from Haiti who fought at the battle of October 9, 1779, in the failed attempt to liberate Savannah from British rule. The drummer boy represents Henri Christophe, who served in that battle and later went on to fight for the abolition of slavery and Haitian independence from France.

sculpted the drummer boy in the statue to represent Christophe at the time of battle.

At some time in the 1780s, Christophe purchased his freedom and later went on to become a major leader in the Haitian wars for abolition of slavery and independence from France. Biographers note that Christophe's military experience in the *Chasseurs-Volontaires* contributed to his later success as a revolutionary general and political leader. Christophe later ruled over northern Haiti for fourteen years.

Although the participation of this unit in the struggle for American independence from Britain is very clearly taught in schools in Haiti, the episode has been little remembered in American textbooks or historical studies, or taught in schools. For this reason, the establishment of the monument was a moment

of pride for Haitians, and the 2010 unveiling of the monument was attended by representatives of the Haitian American community and of the Haitian government as well.

Panels on the sides of the monument give details about Christophe and the *Chasseurs-Volontaires*. The monument was funded with contributions from the Haitian American community, who celebrated the recognition of their contribution to the American struggle for independence.

GEORGIA HUSSARS MONUMENT

The Georgia Hussars Monument is simply a mounted cannon from the eighteenth century, commemorating the unit of mounted rangers organized by James Oglethorpe in 1736. The cannon is found on Bay Street, just to the east of the Cotton Exchange Building. The

Hussars Monument. This simple cannon on display on Bay Street honors the Georgia Hussars, a unit that fought in the American Revolution and continues today as a part of the Georgia National Guard.

gun itself is a British six-pounder cannon, apparently abandoned during the American Revolution in the Siege of Savannah, found while excavating a sidewalk in 1958.

The term "Hussar," derived from the Hungarian language, was widely used in the eighteenth century to describe light cavalry units in many countries. The unit known as the Georgia Hussars fought at the July 7, 1742, Battle of Bloody Marsh, against Spanish troops from Florida in the War of Jenkins' Ear, and again during the Revolutionary War in the Siege of Savannah in 1779.

The unit continued through the nineteenth century, participating in the War with Mexico and the Civil War, as a unit of the Fifth Georgia Cavalry in the Confederate service. Congress disbanded all militias in the states of the former Confederacy in 1867, and members

of the former Hussars set up a civilian group called the "Savannah Sabre Club," which held social events, marched in parades, and held marksmanship competitions. On May 23, 1872, the military unit was formally revived. In later years the Georgia Hussars (as the 108th Cavalry Regiment of the Georgia State National Guard) served in Mexico, World War I, World War II, Korea, Vietnam, Desert Storm, Bosnia and Herzegovina, and Operation Enduring Freedom in Afghanistan.

FORT WAYNE AND OLD FORT JAMES JACKSON

Among the fort sites near Savannah are two close to the downtown that played a role in the defense of the city in the American Revolution and the War of 1812, Fort Wayne and Fort James Jackson (or "Old Fort Jackson"), both to the east of Savannah, facing the approach to the city up the Savannah River from the Atlantic.

Just east of the downtown section of Savannah is a large brick structure, now part of the city's waterworks, and once the site of Fort Wayne. The fort dates back to the mid-eighteenth century, when a wooden gun emplacement was built near the site of the Trustees' Garden and known as "Fort Halifax." After the British victory in Savannah in 1779, British military engineers expanded the existing Fort Halifax and renamed it Fort Prevost. Much of the work was done by slave labor under the direction of British governor James Wright.

At the end of the Revolution, Fort Halifax was renamed "Fort Wayne" in honor of the American Patriot general Anthony Wayne. Wayne was originally from Pennsylvania and had served in the American Revolution in several campaigns, where his personality earned him the nickname "Mad Anthony." After the Revolution, like General Greene, he settled in Georgia on lands granted to him by the state in recognition of his service in the Revolution. However, as noted in the previous chapter, the only surviving evidence of Fort Wayne is the imposing fort-like wall of the city waterworks, just to the east of the Trustees' Garden site.

"Old Fort Jackson" is a well-maintained historic site about two miles east of Savannah, accessible from East President Street by way of Woodcock Street and Fort Jackson Road. It has been restored to its appearance during the Civil War, although it represented part of the British defenses of Savannah in the earlier Revolutionary period as well.

Brass Gun at Fort Jackson. This gun looks east along the Savannah River from Fort Jackson, showing the defenses of the city from possible attack by ships coming from the Atlantic.

WILLIAM JASPER MONUMENT

Madison Square (intersection of Bull and Harris Streets)

A statue memorializing one of the heroes of the American Revolution is the Sergeant Jasper Monument, erected in 1880, 101 years after his death. Located in the center of Madison Square, the dramatic bronze statue sculpted by Alexander Doyle shows William Jasper holding aloft the battle flag of the South Carolina Continentals while under fire. William Jasper, born in South Carolina, first earned fame for raising the battle flag with the crescent moon after it had been shot down during the British attack on Sullivan's Island, near Charleston, on June 28, 1776. On October 9, 1779, in the Siege of Savannah, Jasper again raised the battle flag of the South Carolina Continentals at the Spring Hill Redoubt in Savannah, where he was shot and killed.

William Jasper Monument. This monument in Madison Square depicts Sergeant William Jasper, who raised the banner of the South Carolina Second Regiment of Continentals, both in defense of Fort Moultrie (near Charleston) and in the attack of Patriot forces on British-held Savannah, where he was fatally wounded. He was one of very few enlisted men remembered as a hero of the American Revolution.

Through the nineteenth century, many paintings, prints, and other memorials of the heroic actions of William Jasper were produced, and he remains one of the most-remembered or celebrated heroes of the American Revolution, particularly in the South. He is one of very few of enlisted rank (rather than officers) from that war who have been specifically honored with monuments.

The panels on three sides of the monument depict scenes from Jasper's life—his mounting the flag on Sullivan's Island near Charleston, freeing Patriot prisoners from British captivity at a spring just west of Savannah, and the battle in Savannah when he was fatally wounded. A granite marker shows the British positions in the Savannah battle.

JASPER SPRINGS MONUMENT, JASPER SPRINGS PARK

Sergeant Jasper's legendary rescue of Patriot prisoners has a separate memorial just west

Jasper Springs. This marble monument takes note of the legend that Sergeants William Jasper and John Newton liberated twelve American prisoners from the British at the spring that lies just behind the monument.

of the city about three miles from City Hall, in a tiny park that marks the historic spot. The monument was put up in 1932 and funded by the federal government, sponsored by a local chapter of the Daughters of the American Revolution. The monument is a stone monolith set up on a granite base, with granite steps that descend into a spring-fed pool, and covered with a wooden pavilion. It was on this site that Sergeant William Jasper and Sergeant John Newton are said to have rescued twelve Patriot prisoners from the British in August 1779. The park and monument can be reached from downtown by way of East Bay Street or by the Augusta Road exit from Interstate 516; the monument is just west of the interstate.

A nearby marker makes note of the fact that the story of Jasper's rescue of prisoners traces to Parson Weems, who recorded many otherwise undocumented legends of the Colonial and Revolutionary periods.

FIRST AFRICAN BAPTIST CHURCH

23 Montgomery Street
(912) 233-6597
Note that tours are available on Wednesdays. Phone for hours and fees.

First African
Baptist Church.

The First African Baptist Church building facing Franklin Square itself was constructed in 1859, but the congregation dates back to 1788, founded by Reverend George Liele. The First African Baptist Church is considered the oldest African American church congregation in the United Sates. Those who established this church in 1859 were mostly slaves, and they split away from the original congregation, taking the name "First African Baptist Church" with them to their location on Franklin Square.

Guides point out several aspects of the church relating to its use as a "station" on the Underground Railroad, by which escaped slaves sought to escape to freedom. Holes in the floorboards, arranged in an African pattern, reputedly were drilled to allow air for fugitives hiding under the floorboards. A unique pattern in the ceiling, reflecting a "nine patch quilt," signifies a place of rest or refuge. A tunnel leading from the church either to a nearby escape route by way of another building or to the river may have once existed, but it has not been located. The pews themselves are original and were constructed by slaves.

This historic church was used as a meeting place for Savannah African American activists in the civil rights movement of the 1950s and 1960s. Reverend Ralph Gilbert of the church worked with civil rights activist William Wesley Law in organizing demonstrations.

FIRST BRYAN BAPTIST CHURCH

575 Bryan Street

Members of the original First Baptist Congregation continued as "First Bryan Baptist Church" named after Andrew Bryan, a former slave who had purchased his freedom and who had purchased a site for the church at 575 Bryan Street, now in the Yamacraw Village section of Savannah. That site is regarded as the oldest continually black-owned parcel of land in the United States.

WASHINGTON GUNS

Located in a small shelter on Bay Street, just to the east of City Hall, are two well-preserved cannons. These two guns were presented to the Chatham Artillery unit of the city of Savannah by George Washington during his

Washington Guns. George Washington presented these two guns to the Chatham Artillery after they hosted him during his visit to Savannah in 1791. They are displayed in a small shelter on Bay Street just east of City Hall.

visit to the city in 1791. The guns had been captured from British positions at the Battle of Yorktown at the end of the American Revolution. According to local legend, Washington was impressed by an honorary twenty-six-gun artillery salute by the Chatham Artillery and presented the guns as a return gesture. One is an English gun manufactured in 1758 during the reign of King George II; the other was made in Strasburg, France, in 1756.

The nearby historical marker explains that the English six-pounder has the motto of the Order of the Garter on the barrel. The motto

Chatham Artillery Monument. This monument in Emmet Park between Bay Street and Factors Walk is dedicated to the Chatham Artillery, one of the oldest military units in the United States and still active.

is *Honi soit qui mal y pense* ("Shame to him who thinks evil of it"). The French gun, cast in Strasburg in 1756, has the coat of arms of King Louis XIV, known as the "Sun King." The gun has an engraving of the sun, a Latin phrase meaning "The Last Argument of Kings," and dolphins, which served as emblems of the kings of France from as early as 1350.

The guns were buried during the Civil War to prevent their capture by Union forces, and they were dug up after the war in 1872. Neither has been fired since 1961, when one was damaged during a demonstration firing. A small monument to the Chatham Artillery unit is found in Emmet Park.

CHATHAM ARTILLERY PUNCH

There are several stories explaining the origin of this famous drink, as well as several different recipes. One story favored in Savannah is that the drink originated during the visit of George Washington to Savannah in 1791. According to that legend, when Washington donated the two cannons to the Chatham Artillery, the military unit responded by giving him a reception at which the punch was first served. Among the many recipes for the punch are several that describe filling a horse bucket with crushed ice, and then adding gallons of Catawba wine, with whole bottles of champagne, rum, gin, and whiskey, cut (somewhat) with tea, as well as lemon and other fruit juice. That legend (and the exact recipe itself) has been difficult to document with certainty.

One account comes from an 1885 article in the *Augusta Chronicle* that claims the punch was the invention of A. H. Luce, a bartender attending a visit between the Republican Blues and the Chatham Artillery, two local social clubs organized around military units. A more likely story stems from a visit to Savannah by journalists in the 1880s, at which a strong punch was served, featuring some of those same ingredients, leading to every member of the party passing out. Rumors and stories spread after that period, with a variety of recipes calling for roughly the same list of ingredients. Newspaper accounts over the next decades offered some documentation, leaving specialists in "mixology" with even more recipes and legends.

The name of the punch and the legend that it was served during Washington's visit make the drink a kind of Savannah "artifact" of the early national period.

OLD CITY EXCHANGE BELL AND CUPOLA

Located on the north side of East Bay Street just east of Drayton Street is a small cupola containing a bell. The bell is believed to be the oldest in the state of Georgia, cast in 1802 in Austria and installed in 1803 on the top of the City Exchange Building that had been built in 1790. A watchman in the tower was hired to ring the bell when fires were spotted. At its elevated spot in a small cupola, it was sounded to announce important visitors, including the Marquis de Lafayette and Presidents Monroe, Polk, and Fillmore, or to announce major events. As the highest point in the city, a cupola over the bell had provided a popular lookout to watch for expected arrival of ships or significant visitors.

In 1902, the City Exchange Building was torn down and replaced with the present City Hall; the bell was installed at first by the Rourke Iron Works, where the company maintained it until 1940. In that year, a hurricane brought down the company's tower. Walter Lee Mingledorff, founder of a local air-conditioning company, acquired the bell and gave it to the Chamber

Old City Exchange Bell. Mounted in this little cupola near the Cotton Exchange, the 1803 Old City Exchange Bell is carefully preserved. In the early 1800s the bell served as the city alarm of danger or to announce major celebrations.

of Commerce. In 1957, the replica cupola was built to protect the bell from the weather, with funding from the Savannah Chamber of Commerce, the Savannah-Chatham Historic Site and Monument Commission, and the Pilot Club of Savannah. The bell and cupola are directly across Bay Street from the Chamber of Commerce Building, which had earlier housed the Cotton Exchange.

OTHER MONUMENTS OF INTEREST—AMERICAN REVOLUTION AND EARLY NATIONAL PERIOD

SIEGE OF SAVANNAH MONUMENT BATTLEFIELD PARK, OFF LOUISVILLE ROAD

East of the replica fort at the Battlefield Park is a stone marker on a slightly raised mound describing the battle site.

BUTTON GWINNETT MONUMENT, COLONIAL PARK CEMETERY

Set up in 1964, this monument in Colonial Park Cemetery is in recognition of Button Gwinnett, who was one of three signers of the Declaration of Independence who represented Georgia. Gwinnett was killed in a duel with a political rival, Lachlan McIntosh, in 1777. The monument is made of veined Georgia marble, and it has four columns set on a marble base that hold up a flat slab that forms a roof over the monument. The name "Button Gwinnett" is carved in the edge of this slab and also appears in the form of a signature on the tablet mounted on the marble pedestal under the roof. The large monument also marks Gwinnett's nearby grave site.

Button Gwinnett Monument. In the Colonial Park Cemetery, this monument marks the grave of a Georgia signer of the Declaration of Independence, who was later killed in a duel.

3 Antebellum Period, 1816–1860

Savannah became one of the great centers of Southern cultural, economic, social, and political life in the antebellum or pre–Civil War period.

The forty-five-year antebellum period was later glorified in sentimental historical fiction. The harsh realities of the expanding slave system were often glossed over in novels, short stories, poetry, and song and by civic leaders and historical writers who stressed a sugarcoated view of the genteel life of the prosperous slaveholders. Although slave owners had a financial incentive to ensure that slaves were healthy and well fed, the injustices and cruelties of the system were obvious to some visitors, and locals as well, and during the antebellum decades the system led to increasing political conflict between the slaveholding regions and the "free" states of the North and West.

The prosperous, elite class of plantation slave owners dominated Southern political, cultural, and intellectual life through these decades. Several of the great cities of the South, such as Richmond, Atlanta, Charleston, and New Orleans as well as Savannah, flourished in this period, with the building of elegant town homes and mansions, theaters, schools, churches, and colleges, accompanied by a rich intellectual and artistic life shared by planters and supporting businessmen, lawyers, and other professionals. The wealthiest plantation owners often maintained town homes in these cities, as well as homes at their cotton, rice, sugar, or tobacco plantations in nearby rural regions. Artisans, craftsmen, architects, and artists, hired by the wealthy planters,

left a legacy of beautiful buildings in homes, churches, and other civic buildings.

Cultural life thrived, supported and shared by the elite groups, so that Southern cities saw the flourishing of the arts, including not only architecture but also furnishings, ironwork, painting, printing, theater, and writing. Meanwhile, most slaves lived in miserable conditions, worked long hours, and received only bare subsistence food and housing from their owners.

During the Civil War, several Southern cities were virtually destroyed by fire, including Augusta and Atlanta in Georgia and Richmond in Virginia, but among those that survived almost undamaged by the war was Savannah. In Savannah, nearly one hundred homes and other buildings have been identified as surviving examples of the antebellum period. Many have undergone extensive remodeling and modernization, but even so, the look of whole streets in Savannah echoes the antebellum period.

Like other Southern metropolises, Savannah hosted town houses owned by planters whose out-of-town plantations and crews of slaves generated wealth for the owners. Those planters relied on bankers and brokers or factors to manage the sale of cotton and rice and other business matters. Lawyers, bankers, and other professionals also built elegant mansions.

Savannah Grey Brick

Many of the homes built in the antebellum period in Savannah made use of local "Savannah grey brick." It was so called because it was made from grey clay found on the plantation of Henry McAlpin, "The Hermitage," that was located on the banks of the Savannah River about a mile west of Savannah. McAlpin's plantation was the only one of several upriver Savannah River plantations in the antebellum period that was based mostly on industry, rather than raising a crop.

In addition to his brick business, McAlpin ran a foundry and a steam-powered lumber mill, as well as rice fields along the river. All were operated by slaves, and McAlpin was one of Georgia's largest slave owners, with some 188 slaves at the time of his death in 1851.

The plantation and its factories have long ago disappeared. In 1935, the land was purchased by the Union Camp Corporation that set up a pulp and paper mill on the site. The mill flourished from making grocery bags, and it is now owned by International Paper. The plantation home itself was disassembled and reconstructed by Henry Ford at Richmond Hill, Georgia, in the mid-1930s. Richmond Hill is about fifteen miles south of Savannah near the site of Fort McAllister. Ford financed the preservation and reconstruction of the fort.

Today the rare Savannah grey bricks are a valuable commodity because of the demand for use in restoration of older properties in Savannah, or for special projects such as fireplaces or walls, with individual brick prices running from $2.50 to $4.00.

Cobblestone pavement. Along the ramps to River Street and on River Street itself, the stone pavement was made from ballast stones from thousands of sailing ships that dumped the stones in Savannah during the antebellum period in order to take on export cargo.

Below the bluffs, along River Street, the city docks saw thriving port activity where products of plantations were brought by wagon or riverboat, or after 1835, by ox- or horse-drawn heavy wagons from the railway station several blocks away. The freight was then unloaded, stored, and reloaded aboard oceangoing ships for transport to points of purchase in New England and Europe. River Street held so many financial and commercial buildings that it became known as the "Wall Street of the South."

The very street paving along River Street serves as a kind of "monument" to this era, noted in historical markers along the waterfront. When ships arrived "in ballast"— that is, without a heavy cargo but weighed down with loads of stones—stevedores would unload the ballast before packing the ships with cotton or other exports. These stones themselves made excellent paving, and the "cobblestones" of River Street and the ramps leading up to Bay Street are ballast from sailing ships of 150–200 years ago. Ballast stones were also used in retaining walls and buildings near the waterfront.

SITES

COLONIAL PARK CEMETERY (1750–1855)

Entrance: corner of Abercorn and Oglethorpe Streets

Colonial Park Cemetery, squarely in the Historic District of Savannah, is open from 8:00 a.m. to 5:00 p.m., and until 8:00 p.m. in the months of March through November. Some ghost tours operate in the cemetery in the evening hours.

The cemetery was originally set up in 1750, by Christ Church, and served as a public cemetery until 1855. No one is exactly sure

Colonial Park Cemetery gate. The gate to the Colonial Park Cemetery at Oglethorpe and Bull Streets was erected by the Daughters of the American Revolution in 1913 although the cemetery had closed to burials in the 1850s.

how many graves the cemetery contains. A careful archeological study by the Chicora Foundation completed in 1999 identified "at least" 9,238 marked and unmarked burials.

Although the cemetery was administered by the city in the early nineteenth century, very poor records were kept and no exact plan was followed. As a consequence, graves soon became difficult to identify, stones were often moved, and even the exact boundaries of the cemetery remained unclear.

Among the many legends associated with the cemetery is the tale of intentional vandalism by Union soldiers during their occupation of Savannah in 1865. Using their bayonets, the soldiers reputedly altered a number of birth and death dates on headstones. Some of these altered stones, along with others from long-lost graves, can now be seen mounted on a brick wall on the southeast corner of the cemetery, close to East Perry Lane.

One notable feature of the cemetery is a number of brick vaults or aboveground tombs. Presumably the vaults were constructed of brick due to the fact it was readily available and far cheaper than granite or marble. Both regular red/orange bricks and locally produced grey bricks can be seen in some of these vaults.

When the body of General Nathanael Greene was disinterred in 1901 to be reburied at the base of the monument in Johnson Square, no one was sure at first exactly which body in the Greene family tomb was his. A small metal plaque and remains of clothing helped identify the bodies of General Greene and his son. The two bodies were removed from the family tomb (the patched brick tombs today show their removal), and both were reburied at the site of the monument.

Numerous duels were fought in the cemetery, and several of the gravestones make note of the fact that the deceased died in a duel. A historical marker describes the prevalence of duels in early Savannah. Many other historical markers in the cemetery give details of the lives of significant figures buried there.

Mutilated gravestones. Along the southeast wall of the Colonial Park Cemetery, these mutilated, eroded, or abandoned tombstones have been mounted in a unique display.

Brick tombs. These tombs made of brick are quite rare and are characteristic of Savannah's Colonial Park Cemetery.

THE INTERNATIONAL SEAMEN'S HOUSE (1830s–PRESENT)

25 Houston Street

This relatively modern-looking building houses an organization with a long history in Savannah and in the ports of the world. The Seamen's House traces its ancestry back to the "Bethel movement" that began in Britain in 1814 and in New York in 1821. The move to reform the conditions of mariners and to bring religious messages to them was one of several early to mid-nineteenth-century social reform movements. Those included overseas Christian mission work, abolition of slavery, abstinence from alcohol, votes for women, and prison reform.

Dedicated to ministering to the spiritual and physical needs of the ocean's mariners, the Bethel movement set up "seamen's houses"

in port cities throughout the North Atlantic and later around the world. These facilities provided ministers and social services to visiting crews while in port. The first facility in Savannah as part of this movement was the Penfield Mariner's Church, set up in 1831.

That church was funded by money left by Josiah Penfield, who had been a local Baptist deacon. The Penfield Mariner's Church was on East Bay Street, between Lincoln and Abercorn Streets. The church operated until 1843, when several Savannah churches set up the Savannah Port Society to continue ministries to visiting seamen. The society went on to establish a boardinghouse for visiting sailors in 1850 and a seamen's "Bethel," or church and social service building, that operated at various locations until 1965, when the present International Seamen's House and Chapel at 25 Houston Street opened.

International Seamen's House. Descended from an organization founded in the 1830s, the International Seamen's House continues to offer social services to mariners from around the world.

Oyster-shell pavement. Next to the Seamen's House, this unique oyster-shell pavement is one of many representing different eras of Savannah's history.

In recent years, the continuing organization, the Savannah Port Society, provides religious services (Catholic and Protestant) to thousands of visiting seamen. Modern social services offered include transportation for shopping and medical needs, telephone services, internet access, donated clothing, literature, and media resources, all free of charge to American and international seafarers.

Visitors at the International Seamen's House may notice the unique oyster-shell pavement on East St. Julian Street, which runs next to the Seamen's House. Among the many and varied historical pavements of the city, this two-block section of oyster-shell aggregate is unique.

SAVANNAH CUSTOM HOUSE (1845–1852)

On the corner of East Bay and Bull Streets is the Savannah Custom House. Two earlier U.S. Custom Houses in Savannah had burned down, so, in 1845, the U.S. government purchased the lot and construction began on the site. The site was already historic, since a wooden home occupied by James Oglethorpe had once stood there and John Wesley had preached his first sermon in the colony of Georgia at the tabernacle on the rear of the plot of land.

The granite and masonry Custom House was designed to be fireproof by architect John S.

Custom House. Completed in 1852, the Savannah Custom House was the site of a famous slave ship case as well as the site at which an elected convention voted for Georgia to secede from the United States in January 1861.

Norris. Completed in 1852, the building housed not only custom officials but also the U.S. Post Office as well as federal courts. In 1860, a famous case against a slave ship, the *Wanderer*, was tried and won in the court (though the owners were later acquitted in a jury trial).

On January 19, 1861, following the election of Abraham Lincoln and the passage of resolutions of secession from the United States by South Carolina, Florida, Mississippi, and Alabama, an elected state convention met in the Savannah Custom House and voted for Georgia to also secede. The Custom House remained under Confederate control until General William Tecumseh Sherman led Union troops into Savannah in December 1864.

THE SORREL-WEED HOUSE (1835–1840)

Bull and Harris Streets, 6 West Harris, north side of Madison Square

The home is open for tours, managed by the Historic Savannah Foundation. Phone number for hours and fees: (912) 257-2223.

The building was originally built over the period 1835–1840, and it is the largest surviving home in Savannah of the era. The original owner was Francis Sorrel, a prosperous shipping merchant. Among the sons of Francis Sorrel was Gilbert Moxley Sorrel, who served as a general in the Confederate army, the youngest of that rank. Confederate general Robert E. Lee was a personal friend of Francis Sorrel who visited the Sorrel home several times, and General Lee helped advance the career of young Gilbert Sorrel.

The home was sold in 1859 to another local business owner, Henry D. Weed, who did not take possession until after 1862. The Weed family retained the house until 1914. After going through several remodels, the

The Sorrel-Weed House.

building was carefully restored in 1999 to the original layout, including an elegant stairway to the second floor and a front dining area divided by pillars into a private and more public space. Because of the long period of ownership by the Weed family, the home is usually identified as the "Sorrel-Weed" House.

The house has earned a reputation as one of the most haunted in Savannah and, according to some accounts, one of the most haunted in the United States. The foundation that operates the house offers evening ghost tours for a separate fee. Phenomena reported include sightings of figures in the windows, the feeling of being touched by an invisible figure, unexplained nausea, failure of electronic equipment, and sounds of disembodied voices. Most Savannah ghost tours and ghost guides include accounts of paranormal events in the house. The original events that reputedly sparked the ghost tales included the suicide of Matilda Sorrel, the wife of the first owner of the building, as well as the mysterious death of a slave girl with whom Francis Sorrel presumably had an affair. Other investigators have suggested that the paranormal experiences stem from the possibility that many of the deaths of Patriot forces during the attack on British-held Savannah in October 1779 occurred near the site of the building.

SS *SAVANNAH* MONUMENT AND SCARBOROUGH HOUSE

In 1819, the sail-and-steam ship *Savannah* successfully made the trip from Savannah to Liverpool, England, partially under steam power, on a twenty-seven-day trip. This voyage was the first crossing of the Atlantic Ocean by a steamship and heralded the great changes in ocean transportation that would come over the next decades. Captained by Moses Rodgers, and financed by local entrepreneurs, including businessman William Scarborough of the shipping firm Scarborough and Isaacs, the ship made the crossing mostly under sail power. On the voyage, in two separate incidents, sailors aboard other ships spotted the smoke from the SS *Savannah* and gave chase, assuming that it was a sailing vessel that had caught fire. The ship went on to visit ports in the Baltic Sea, including St. Petersburg in Russia, before returning to Savannah.

The ship had several unique features, including side-mounted paddlewheels that could be raised and stored on deck. Since steam power was in its infancy, no one booked passage on the voyage across the Atlantic, for fear of a boiler explosion. News reports called it a "steam coffin." However,

the ship made the two 1819 crossings of the Atlantic, outward bound and return, safely.

The round trip to Europe and back were the only voyages across the Atlantic made by the ship, and it would be another twenty-nine years before another American-built and American-owned steamship made the crossing. By the 1830s, British and other European companies had built sail-and-steam ships, and such "hybrid" steamships began making regular crossings by the 1840s and 1850s. The *Savannah* itself went into coastal service for two years before running aground and wrecking on Long Island, New York, in 1821.

Although the businessmen of Savannah did not follow up with another steamship, the pathbreaking voyage of the SS *Savannah* was a major historic event. Steam transportation by sea would revolutionize world trade; together with rail transport on land, the new mechanical systems became hallmarks of nineteenth-century technical progress.

The Ships of the Sea Museum at 41 Martin Luther King Boulevard is housed in the elegant home of William Scarborough, one of the major backers of the SS *Savannah.* The museum shows ship models, paintings, and maritime antiques, and the house itself serves as a memorial to the pioneering role of the city in maritime transport. The collections of maritime art and artifacts focus primarily on the age of sail and early steamships, but they also include a room devoted to the sinking of the passenger liner *Titanic* after striking an iceberg on April 15, 1912.

Today a small monument to the SS *Savannah* is found on River Street, at the foot of Barnard Street, in the form of a model of the ship in the midst of a fountain. The nearby marker also describes the steamboat SS *Randolph*,

Scarborough House.

SS *Savannah* Monument. The SS *Savannah*, funded and launched from the city, was the first sail-and-steam ship to cross the Atlantic Ocean.

an iron-hulled ship that operated successfully as a riverboat. That steamboat was built in Britain and shipped disassembled to the United States, where it was put together and then served for years as a riverboat, the first iron-hulled ship or boat in the United States.

ST. VINCENT'S ACADEMY

207 East Liberty Street

The origins of St. Vincent's Academy, located next to the Cathedral of St. John the Baptist, resulted from the work of the Sisters of Mercy, a religious order first set up in Ireland in 1831 by Sister Catherine McCauley. In 1841, the first group of Sisters of Mercy came to the

United States from Ireland to set up schools and infirmaries for poor and sick immigrants. Four years later, in 1845, six Sisters of Mercy from Charleston, South Carolina, led by Father Jeremiah Francis O'Neill, established St. Vincent's Academy in Savannah to serve as a secondary school for girls. At first the school was located on the corner of Abercorn and Liberty Streets, operating as both a private school and an orphanage. Boarding facilities for students were added a few years later.

The sisters named the school after the sixteenth-century cleric St. Vincent de Paul, who was known as the "Apostle of Charity." By the 1850s and 1860s, the school operated simultaneously as an orphanage, a boarding school, a day school, and a free school. The St. Vincent's Convent soon took the lead as a motherhouse in Georgia, establishing more than twenty orphanages, schools, and hospitals in the state. The president of the Confederacy, Jefferson Davis, sent two of his children to the school in Savannah.

The original building itself was designed by the architect Charles B. Cluskey (c. 1808–1871), in the Greek Revival style. Cluskey was responsible for a number of other Savannah buildings, including the Sorrell-Weed House, as well as other notable buildings across Georgia.

Since 1919, the school has been operated as a Catholic secondary day school for girls. In recent years the enrollment has been about 350 students. The school continues to honor Sister Catherine McCauley, with an annual award in her name given to one or two alumnae who embody the values of St. Vincent's Academy and the life of the order's founder.

FACTORS WALK

Immediately behind the buildings that front on River Street is Factors Walk, unique to

Factors Walk Bridge. Throughout the antebellum period and even later, cotton factors used these walkways as they strolled from office to office, managing Georgia's cotton exports.

Savannah. A series of walkways and iron bridges connect the third story of the buildings on River Street, at the level of Bay Street. East Factors Walk runs from City Hall to East Broad Street, while West Factors Walk runs from City Hall west to Montgomery Street.

These bridges and walkways connected the cotton warehouses and factors' offices that faced the river. The large brick buildings housed cotton and cotton bales for shipment in warehouses on the first floor, River Street level, while the second and third floors, facing the Walk, housed the offices of the cotton factors or brokers. The cotton factors arranged the purchase of cotton, serving as middlemen between the planters and the buyers placing orders that originated in Britain or in New England, where the cotton textile mills were located through the nineteenth century.

Today Factors Walk, both East and West, provides access to several waterfront hotels that

Driving on River Street

Drivers should be aware that River Street is cobbled and is one-way eastbound, with a streetcar track laid in the cobbles. Because of the cobblestones, tracks, unloading trucks, and many pedestrians, speeds above the legal speed limit of fifteen miles an hour are hazardous. Although there are parking lots on the river side of River Street, at the height of tourist travel, parking is difficult to find, so it may be best to access River Street, with its shops and restaurants, by foot.

have been constructed inside the renovated old warehouses, as well as a wide variety of shops, offices, and restaurants. Cobblestone access ramps for auto and truck traffic from Bay Street down to River Street are found just east of Jefferson Street, east and west of Drayton Street, and at Houston Street on the east. Pedestrian steps from Factors Walk

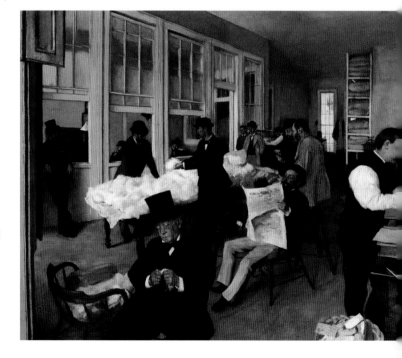

Cotton factors at work. This painting by Edgar Degas, titled *A Cotton Office in New Orleans*, shows a scene that was probably very typical of the cotton factors' offices in Savannah before and after the Civil War.

MUSÉE DE BEAUX-ARTS, PARIS

River Street. Today, River Street is a bustling attraction of shops and restaurants that occupy the former cotton warehouses that face the waterfront.

down to the River Street level are found at four locations: Barnard Street, just east of City Hall, and at Abercorn and Lincoln Streets.

OLD HARBOR LIGHT (1858)

At the eastern end of Emmet Park, which runs between East Bay Street and Factors Walk, stands the "Old Harbor Light." With the appearance of a decorative streetlight, it was originally a guide to navigation, as the "Rear Range Light."

J. F. Gilmer, captain of engineers, made the original recommendation to the U.S. Lighthouse Board for the light in October 1855, suggesting "a harbor beacon on 'the bay' [in the] city of Savannah, as an aid to vessels approaching the city at night." His recommendation led to the erection of the light in 1858.

The light was one of a pair, with the "Front Range Light" across the Savannah River on Fig Island. The two lights helped guide ships into the Savannah harbor, past the hulks of six ships that had been scuttled in the river by the British to prevent Patriot forces from sailing upriver aboard French ships. By 1880, the range lights to guide ships both on Fig Island and in Savannah were relocated, with the South Range Light installed on the top of the Cotton Exchange Building. However, by this time, the Old Range Light, with its appearance as a giant streetlight in Emmet Park, had become a landmark, and it was simply left in place.

One hundred years after being first installed, the light was in bad shape, with rust and corrosion damage to the lamppost due to the salty and humid river air. The Trustees'

Old Harbor Light. Erected in the 1850s as a guide to navigation, the Old Harbor Light, which resembles a streetlamp on a high post, is a favorite symbol of old Savannah.

Garden Club refurbished Emmet Park and grew concerned about the deterioration of the light. In the late 1990s, the whole structure had become unstable; cables were installed to prevent collapse, and the gaslight was turned off.

Restoration of the lamp became part of a $3 million project to restore and preserve more than forty of the city's monuments in the year 2000, in a project called "Celebrate 2000." Among the other monuments restored in this effort were the Tomochichi marker in Wright Square and the Pulaski Monument.

With $62,500 grants from both the CSX Corporation and the local newspaper (the *Savannah Morning News*) and smaller grants from other businesses, the lamp was taken down and carefully repaired and restored. Rust was removed, and a coating to prevent lightning strikes was added. It was then reconnected to the gas mains so that it could be lit. Ship anchors were installed at the base. Work was completed in January 2001, restoring the old light, which had become one of the iconic symbols of old Savannah.

ANTEBELLUM SAVANNAH STREETSCAPES OF PRIVATE HOMES (1840s–1850s)

Several neighborhoods or blocks in Savannah are notable for representing the decades of construction during the antebellum period. Although these are private residences now and not open to visitors, their preservation and restoration, collectively, give a good sense of the architecture and styles of the antebellum decades. There are many neighborhoods or rows of houses that reflect various periods scattered through the Historic District.

Among the many restored houses from the antebellum period is the row at 443–453 Barnard Street. Known as the "Gordon Block" or "Gordon Row" at the southeast corner of Gordon and Barnard Streets, there is a whole block of fifteen restored row homes from the 1850s, notable for their exterior front staircases.

Gordon Row. Among many antebellum streets that have been preserved and restored, the "Gordon Row," a group of fifteen restored homes, beginning at the southeast corner of Chatham Square, is a prime example.

THE MASSIE HERITAGE CENTER (1856)

201–213 Gordon Street, on Calhoun Square
(912) 395-5070

This building was designed by architect John S. Norris and completed in 1856. The unusual structure has connecting passageways between three separate buildings and was designed as a school for poor children. The name of the building is derived from a bequest left for that purpose by Peter Massie in 1841. The building was used as a school for 133 years, the longest continuously operated school in the state of Georgia.

Operated today as a museum by the Savannah-Chatham County Public School System, the building features several themes, including details of state and local history. One exhibit covers the lifestyle of the Native Americans who inhabited the region before the arrival of the first Europeans. Two exhibits focus on architectural history and the styles that have influenced Savannah's buildings; another is a model of the city layout, showing the original plan. A collection of handcrafted ship models documents the evolution of ship design.

The main focus of the museum is on nineteenth-century primary school education, and several of the exhibits are designed to familiarize children with the methods, materials, and furnishings of early schools. A "Heritage Classroom" includes slate boards for practicing handwriting, pupil desks, and a collection of nineteenth-century schoolbooks.

Massie classroom. This classroom in the Massie Heritage Center is one of several displays in the museum that reflect antebellum Savannah; the building was established as a school for the poor with funds from the estate of Peter Massie, and it was opened in the mid-1850s.

THE OGLETHORPE CLUB (1857)

450 Bull Street, facing Forsyth Park

The Oglethorpe Club was originally built in 1857 as a private home and as the consular office for Edmund Molyneux, the British consul at Savannah.

At the end of the Civil War, after Sherman occupied Savannah, U.S. Army general Oliver Howard appropriated the mansion as his headquarters; the general or his staff later made off with some of the owner's wine cellar and library contents and was presented with a bill for $11,000 in damages, equal to about $171,000 in purchasing power in 2018. The Molyneux family retained the home for twenty years after the war, and then they sold it to

former Confederate general Henry Jackson, who lived in the home until his death in 1898. Jackson was famous in his own right as a leading judge and prosecutor and as a U.S. ambassador to Austria in the 1850s and to Mexico in the 1880s.

Jackson dabbled with poetry and had published a small collection in 1850, titled *Tallulah and Other Poems*. His most famous poem immortalized the words "The Red Old Hills of Georgia," a phrase echoed by Dr. Martin Luther King more than a century later in his "I Have a Dream" speech.

The building is now the headquarters of the Oglethorpe Club, the oldest and most prestigious "gentlemen's club" in Georgia, originally founded in 1870.

Oglethorpe Club. Founded in the late 1850s, the Oglethorpe Club is one of the oldest elite men's clubs in the city.

FORSYTH PARK FOUNTAIN (1858)

In the center of Forsyth Park, near the intersection of Bull Street and Gwinnett Street, is one of Savannah's most-photographed signature sites, the Forsyth Park Fountain. A product of mid-nineteenth-century monumental civic decoration, it has survived and been protected by Savannah residents and local authorities for both its beauty and its practical benefits.

The fountain was installed in 1858, and when it first turned on, spectators were surprised to see the waterspouts reach far beyond the fountain's basin and spray the crowd. The reason was a newly installed water main system of the city. Soon, a larger catch basin was installed, and the fountain began serving its purposes—both as an ornamental

attraction at the end of a favorite walking route down Bull Street and as a cooling spray for the park during the summer months.

The design of the Forsyth Park Fountain, drawn from a New York City iron foundry company model, is based on two tiers. On the top is a figure of a woman holding a staff. The upper tier basin is decorated with wading birds and swamp plants, evoking Georgia's extensive low-country marshlands. Over the more than 150 years of the fountain's operation, it has been remodeled and repainted numerous times. Four spouting tritons—the mythical ancient Greek "mermen" who were half-man and half-fish—all carry shell horns that spout water. They were originally mounted on blocks but are now in the basin itself. Swans

Forsyth Park Fountain. Put in place in 1858, the Forsyth Park Fountain is an iconic emblem of Savannah, as well as favorite and cooling gathering spot at the northern end of the park.

and urns were added in the 1870s, and the current white color of the fountain dates to 1935. The fountain was renovated in 1988, partly funded by donations. The names of donors are inscribed in bricks laid around the fountain base.

There are three other nearly identical fountains in the world. One is in Poughkeepsie, New York; a second in Madison, Indiana; and a third in Cuzco, Peru. Each of the four fountains has slightly different features, due to modifications over the years.

The issues that led to the Civil War (or the War between the States, as it is still remembered in much of the South) had been brewing since the first years of American independence as a nation. The persistence of slavery in the United States divided the country into two adversarial sections after 1820, when the Missouri Compromise was passed in Congress.

The election of Lincoln as an antislavery candidate in 1860, with 39.8 percent of the popular vote but a clear electoral college majority, led to the secession of seven states from the Union and their formation of a separate Confederacy. Five weeks after Lincoln's inauguration as president in March 1861, South Carolina troops fired on the federally held Fort Sumter in the harbor of Charleston, and the Civil War began. Four more slaveholding states joined the Confederacy. The war continued for four more years, ending with the surrender of Confederate armies through the spring of 1865.

THE CIVIL WAR IN GEORGIA

Early in the war, U.S. forces occupied some of the Georgia's Sea Islands, including Tybee Island just to the east of Savannah. Fort Pulaski, located across from Tybee Island on Cockspur Island, fell to Union forces in April 1862. Confederate forces held Fort McAllister, about thirty miles to the south of Savannah by road until December 1864. The Union naval blockade shut off almost all trade into the port of Savannah.

SHERMAN AND SAVANNAH

U.S. Army general William T. Sherman's forces took the city of Atlanta, Georgia, in early November 1864 and began their six-week "march to the sea" on November 15. As Union troops marched out of Atlanta, the city was burned, with destruction of 3,200 of the city's 3,600 homes.

Sherman's sixty-two thousand troops became known as "bummers," as they confiscated livestock and goods and burned plantations when they marched toward Savannah through November and December 1864. As they came east over the period of six weeks, residents and civic leaders expected that the city of Savannah would be burned to the ground like the Georgia cities of Atlanta, Cassville, and Rome.

However, on Sherman's direct orders, Savannah was preserved, and, famously, on December 22, 1864, Sherman sent a telegram to President Lincoln from his headquarters in the Green-Meldrim House, at 14 West Macon Street on Madison Square:

To his Excellency, President Lincoln,

I beg to present you as a Christmas gift the city of Savannah with one hundred and fifty (150) heavy guns and plenty of ammunition, and also about twenty-five thousand (25,000) bales of cotton.

W. T. Sherman, Maj-Genl

Union guard at Fort Jackson. A costumed interpreter at Fort Jackson represents the Union army occupation of the fort after troops under General W. T. Sherman took over Savannah in December 1864.

SITES

FORT PULASKI

(912) 786-8182

Fort Pulaski is a half-hour drive east from downtown Savannah by way of U.S. Highway 80, located on Cockspur Island at the mouth of the Savannah River. The fort, maintained by the U.S Park Service, is open daily from 9:00 to 5:00 but closed on major holidays.

During the Civil War, the defeat of Confederate forces at the battle for Fort Pulaski in April 1862 effectively sealed the river approach to Savannah, closing the port as part of the Union blockade.

The fort had been built over the period 1829–1847, one of some thirty-one brick and masonry coastal forts called the "Third System of Fortification." Fort Pulaski had been built to withstand cannon fire, with seven-and-a-half-foot solid brick walls and reinforcing masonry piers, making the walls up to eleven feet thick.

Pulaski and the other Third System forts along the coasts of the United States were strategically placed at approaches to bays, rivers, and inlets to protect American harbors from possible foreign invasion. After its completion, Fort Pulaski was named after Casimir Pulaski, the Polish cavalry officer and prince who had died in the American Patriot attack on British-held Savannah in October 1779.

At the secession of Georgia in 1861, Georgia troops peacefully, but lightly, occupied the fort.

The fort's thick walls were excellent protection against the typical cannon shot carried by naval ships. While heavier guns might be mounted ashore, no land gun emplacements

Fort Pulaski. Fort Pulaski's defenses included earthen embankments, a moat, and a drawbridge, visible here on the right.

Fort Pulaski interior. The embrasures on the south side of Fort Pulaski, like this one, look out toward Tybee Island, where gunfire from superior and very accurate Union artillery won the battle.

could be located closer than Tybee Island, one to two miles away. Even the heavier, land-mounted smoothbore cannons of the pre–Civil War era were ineffective against such thick masonry walls at ranges over a half mile or so. However, the Battle of Fort Pulaski in 1862 demonstrated that this type of masonry fort had become outmoded in the face of some new cannon developments of the 1860s.

Union forces occupied nearby Tybee Island and prepared to take Fort Pulaski in early 1862. When Union general Thomas Sherman (not a close relation to General William Tecumseh Sherman) demanded surrender, Fort Pulaski's Confederate commander, Colonel Charles H. Olmsted, refused. Olmsted had six months' supply of provisions, and, under the guns of the fort, a trickle of blockade-runner commerce had briefly flowed in and out of Confederate-held Savannah in the early months of the war in 1861.

The chief engineering officer on the Union side preparing the attack on Fort Pulaski in 1862 was Quincy Adams Gillmore, who had closely followed the development of *rifled* artillery, which the U.S. Army had been testing since 1859. Gillmore believed that such cannons, with spiraled rifling inside the bore, increasing accuracy and range, would be effective, even at the two-mile range from Tybee Island. Repeated and accurate firing at the same spot on the thick walls, he reasoned, could breach the walls and allow targeting firing into the fort's interior.

Gillmore's commander, General Thomas Sherman, like Confederate colonel Olmsted, was skeptical about whether artillery would be effective against the "impregnable" Third

System Fort Pulaski. Even so, General Sherman agreed to allow a bombardment, preparatory to an assault by troops. Sherman had ten thousand Union troops ready for the attack.

Union forces fired on the fort, using both James Rifled cannons and "Parrott rifles," over a thirty-hour bombardment on April 10–11, 1862. The accurate shelling opened huge holes in the fort's walls, allowing a view through the center courtyard of the fort directly to the magazine, packed with explosives. Recognizing that disaster loomed, Olmsted surrendered the fort, avoiding useless bloodshed on both sides. There were very few casualties on either side, but the fort, with its few hundred defenders, was no match for the huge assault force ready to attack, once the walls had been breached and the magazine was unprotected from Union artillery. Despite the lack of bloodshed, with only one death in the fort and several Union gunners mortally wounded from artillery accidents, the battle was a resounding Union victory, with 363 Confederate officers and men taken prisoner.

Today, park docents and information panels show exactly where and how the wall on the south side of the fort was broken through.

The battle spelled the end of the "Third System of Fortification," one of several Civil War–era developments of weaponry and defense that came out of the new industrial technology of the period. Rifled cannons like those that breached the walls of Fort Pulaski ranked with minefields, early machine guns, tethered observation balloons, ironclad warships, and the first submarines in reshaping the nature of warfare.

Divot at Fort Pulaski. Inside the gun embrasure that was breached by Union fire, guides and explanatory panels identify a chipped-out divot in the brickwork that still remains after the damaged wall was later repaired.

Cannon at Fort McAllister. This cannon at Fort McAllister points toward the line of approach of Union troops on December 13, 1864.

Officers' huts. At Fort McAllister, these replica huts represent quarters erected by the Confederates during their occupation and defense of the fort from attack by river and land.

FORT McALLISTER

3894 Fort McAllister Road
Richmond Hill, GA 31324
(912) 727-2339

This thirty-acre state park is about thirty miles, or forty-five minutes by road, south of downtown Savannah. From exit 90 on Interstate 95 south of Savannah, take Georgia Highway 144 and 144-Spur to Savage Island Road, about twelve miles to Fort McAllister State Park.

An earthen-works fort, McAllister defended the southern approaches to Savannah, with its location on the Ogeechee River. There were two battles at the fort during the Civil War. The first, a series of attacks from January to March 1863, consisted of repeated efforts of Union ships to reduce the earthenware fort with gunfire from ships on the river. The fort's "mud" walls tended to absorb shots and could be easily repaired during the night. Union

admiral Samuel F. Du Pont, although he had recognized the problem, took personal blame for the failure of the attacks.

The Second Battle of Fort McAllister occurred in December 1864, as General William T. Sherman's troops arrived after their "march to the sea" from Atlanta. Sherman recognized that the fort prevented Union ships from ascending the Ogeechee River and kept him from linking up with the U.S. Navy offshore blockade ships. Although his troops had lived off the land by "foraging" on their six-week march through Georgia from Atlanta, they were in need of fresh supplies of ammunition and other military goods that could only be obtained from the offshore Union ships.

Sherman ordered a land attack on Fort McAllister on December 13, 1864. Troops of his own old unit (the Second Division, XV Corps, Army of Tennessee), now under the command of General William Hazen, with four thousand troops, vastly outnumbered the fort's fewer than three hundred Confederate defenders.

Spacing out the attackers so that they would be less vulnerable to artillery fire from the fort, the Union forces marched through *abatis* (brush and trees tangled like barbed wire) and land mines (called "torpedoes" in this period). The Union troops under General Hazen quickly overwhelmed the fort in about fifteen minutes. After the fort surrendered, Hazen ordered the fort's Confederate commander, Major George Wayne Anderson, to personally join the detail doing the mine-clearing. The Union officers regarded the emplacement of land mines as a dishonorable form of warfare, which might seem quite an irony considering Sherman's own, well-earned personal reputation for ruthless warfare.

After Union troops took the fort, Sherman opened communication with the Union navy and reached his decision to occupy Savannah without destroying the city. He had achieved

his mission of crossing Georgia and gaining access to the Atlantic Seaboard and Union naval forces.

The preserved gun emplacements and the replica buildings on the fort site were funded by Henry Ford in the mid-1930s.

GREEN-MELDRIM HOUSE

14 West Macon Street, west side of Madison Square, next to St. John's Episcopal Church (912) 233-3845

This well-preserved home dates back to the 1850s, when it was built over the years 1853–1861 for Charles Green, a prosperous cotton factor and shipowner. The house was designed for Green by New York architect John S. Norris, who worked in Savannah from 1846 to 1861, designing several churches and residences.

The building is most famous for serving as the headquarters to General William T. Sherman, during his occupation of Savannah in December 1864. It was from this headquarters that Sherman sent his famous telegram to Lincoln, offering as a "Christmas present" the city of Savannah, along with twenty-five thousand bales of cotton.

On the owner's death in 1881, his son, Edward Moon Green, inherited the house. Edward Green later sold the house in 1892 to Judge Peter Meldrim, who served as mayor of Savannah from 1897 to 1899. Meldrim was a nationally recognized jurist, and he was selected as president of the American Bar Association in 1915. Judge Meldrim lived in the home until his death in 1933. The house was sold to the neighboring St. John's Episcopal Church in 1943, and the outbuildings of the home now serve as the rectory for the church, while the building is operated as a house museum by the church.

The Pink House in the Civil War

At some point during the Civil War, the Pink House building on Reynolds Square may have served as the residence for General Zebulon York, a Confederate general, joining in Louisiana. York was born in Maine and had moved to Louisiana, where he operated a plantation before the war. After being wounded in the Shenandoah Valley (where he lost an arm), he was assigned the duty of recruiting foreign-born soldiers from among Union troops held as prisoners of war by the Confederacy. By some accounts, he resided in the Pink House while engaged in this work before Sherman occupied Savannah late in 1865.

Green-Meldrim House. This building served as the headquarters for General Sherman after the Union occupation of Savannah in December 1864.

The house is a luxurious example of southern Gothic Revival architectural style. The stuccoed brick exterior walls, the cast-iron fence and portico at the front door, and the fortress-like crenellated parapet on the roof are all characteristics of the Gothic style. Interior features are also striking, including original wood, plaster, and ironwork, along with silver-plated door hardware.

SAVANNAH STATE UNIVERSITY AND REVEREND JAMES SIMMS

In the years immediately following the Civil War, the period known as "Reconstruction" (1865–1876), local area black leaders sought to exercise their rights. Among them was Reverend James Simms, of the First Bryan Baptist Church, elected to the state legislature. Simms ran on a pledge to get black city officials and police hired, but it was more than a century later before his principles were implemented. James Simms was the founder and first "proctor" (dean) of Georgia Industrial College for Colored Youth. Today that institution continues as Savannah State University with its campus on Skidaway Road in south Savannah.

Savannah State University. This predominantly African American university was first headed by Reverend James Simms of the First Bryan Baptist Church, who worked for equal treatment of the races during Reconstruction.

AFRICAN AMERICAN LIBERATION MONUMENT

This statue in Rousakis Riverfront Plaza depicts an African American family of four, liberated from slavery with broken chains at their feet. Sculpted by Savannah College of Art and Design professor Dorothy Spradley (assisted by one of her students, Dan Koster), the monument was installed in 2002. The leading advocate of the African American Monument was local black educator Dr. Abigail Jordan, who headed a committee working with the city government and raising funds for the statue over a decade.

The brief text inscribed on the pedestal of the African American family statue is from

African American Monument. This sculpture at Rousakis Riverfront Plaza commemorates the liberation of African Americans from slavery.

a poem by Maya Angelou (1928–2014), referring to the conditions aboard slave ships and the liberation of African Americans from enslavement. The statue, its inscription, and prominent placement in a high-traffic area led to brief controversies; defenders of the monument argued that its placement where many slaves were unloaded was appropriate.

This monument, along with the Ralph Mark Gilbert Civil Rights Museum at 460 Martin Luther King Boulevard opened in 1996, and the Haitian Memorial formally unveiled in Franklin Square in 2010, represent some of the efforts in modern Savannah to recognize the participation of African Americans in the history of the city and the nation.

BEACH INSTITUTE (1867)

502 East Harris
(912) 234-8000

The Beach Institute dates back to 1867, when it was built and then operated by the American Missionary Association. It was named for Alfred S. Beach, who was editor of the *Scientific American* and a major donor for the purchase of the site. The institute operated as part of an effort by northern philanthropists to fund the teaching of reading and writing to freed African Americans, both adults and children. In 1875, the institute was transferred to the Savannah Board of Education, and it became a free public school for African American children. In 1919, the institute closed as other public schools for black children were opened.

Today the institute is a cultural center, with programs and exhibits focusing on arts and crafts by black artisans and reflecting the African American heritage. One collection is a set of wood carvings by folk artist Ulysses Davis (1913–1990). The building also houses the offices of the King-Tisdell Cottage

The Beach Institute. Established during Reconstruction as part of the effort to bring literacy to liberated African Americans, the institute continues today as a museum and art gallery of African American culture.

Foundation, which owns both the Beach Institute Building and the King-Tisdell Cottage, which is discussed in the next chapter.

Several of the African American History walking tours noted in appendix A include the Beach Institute and the King-Tisdell Cottage, although each can be visited without a guided tour.

BIG DUKE ALARM BELL (1872)

Located in the parkway divider at the intersection of East Oglethorpe Avenue and Abercorn Street is a large alarm bell. Originally installed in 1872 as a fire alarm bell, close to the Fire Department Building still located on Oglethorpe Avenue, the bell was named after Marmaduke ("Big Duke") Hamilton, chairman of the city's fire committee. Marmaduke Hamilton's beautifully restored home is nearby at 116 East Oglethorpe Avenue.

At first used to call out volunteers and to warn of a city fire, the bell was later used as a general warning, to announce major

Big Duke Alarm Bell. This fire alarm bell was first installed during Reconstruction and now serves as a monument to fallen firefighters.

Susan Baker Taylor King

Susan Ann Baker was born a slave on a plantation in Liberty County, Georgia, on August 6, 1848. When she was about seven years old, she and her brother were sent to live with her grandmother in Savannah. There she learned to read, despite the fact that teaching African Americans to read was strictly against the law. She learned from two different black women who secretly operated "schools" on the streets, and then learned more with aid from two white children who repeated their lessons for her.

When the Civil War swept through Georgia, in April 1862, at age fourteen, Susan Baker was sent back to the country to live with her mother. When nearby Fort Pulaski was captured by the Union army on April 12, she and her uncle's family and other African Americans fled to St. Simons Island, then occupied by Union forces. Word of her ability to read and write soon spread, and U.S. Navy commodore Louis Goldsborough, in command of the North Atlantic Blockade Squadron, offered her books and supplies if she would agree to set up a school for the black children living on the island. She agreed, becoming the first African American teacher in Georgia. In the evenings, she would teach adults to read and write. While on St. Simons Island, she met and married Sergeant Edward King, of the South Carolina Volunteers (later renamed the Thirty-Third U.S. Colored Infantry).

From 1862 to the end of the war in 1865, she traveled along with the troops in her husband's unit, serving officially as a laundress and working as a nurse by day and teaching African American soldiers to read and write in the evenings, all without pay. She and Sergeant King returned to Savannah in 1866, where she set up the first school there for freed black children, though she soon had to close it as other schools were established. Edward died from an accident while working on the Savannah waterfront in September 1866.

She began writing her memoirs in 1890 and published them in 1902, under the title Reminiscences of My Life in Camp with the 33rd US Colored Troops. *The book is the only published autobiography of a black woman from the Civil War period. Today, she has been honored in Savannah through adopting her name for one of the four Savannah Belles Ferries, the* Susie King Taylor.

events, or to welcome returning troops. In 1985, the bell was placed here and dedicated as a memorial to all firefighters. In 1993, a plaque was added, inscribed with the names of twenty-five Savannah firefighters and those from nearby communities, and other emergency responders who died in the line of duty. Surrounding the bell are brick pavers, some inscribed with the names of donors who contributed to the cost of the memorial.

In October, on Firefighters' Memorial Day (the Sunday before October 9), ceremonies are held at the bell, with the names of the fallen heroes read aloud, the bell struck once for each, and a flower placed on the memorial stone behind the bell.

CATHEDRAL OF ST. JOHN THE BAPTIST (1876)

222 East Harris Street
(912) 233-4709

The Cathedral of St. John the Baptist is one of the most impressive buildings in Savannah. The Catholic congregation in Savannah dates back to the mid-1790s, when émigrés from Haiti established the first Catholic church in the city. A small frame church was completed in 1799 for the French-speaking refugees, Congrégation de Saint Jean-Baptiste.

After several relocations, in 1870 the present site for the new cathedral was chosen. In that year, Pope Pius IX appointed Rev. Ignatius Persico as the fourth bishop of Savannah, with the diocese covering the state of Georgia. As bishop, Persico worked on plans for the new cathedral, acquiring the present lot from the Sisters of Mercy through a land exchange. Bishop Persico resigned as bishop, and his successor, Fr. William H. Gross, initiated construction of the cathedral in 1873, which was completed and dedicated in 1876. Relatively unusual in the southern

Cathedral of St. John the Baptist. Completed in 1876, the French Gothic–style Catholic cathedral welcomes parishioners and visitors alike on the north side of Lafayette Square.

United States, the cathedral is built in the French Gothic style.

A fire in 1898 swept through this section of the city, destroying the interior of the church. Reconstruction over the next two years included further additions, such as the impressive stained-glass windows imported from the Austrian Tyrol, installed about 1904. A team of artists under the direction of Savannah artist Christopher Murphy painted the murals.

The redecorated and restored cathedral formally opened in 1912. The work from that period and preservation and repairs over the decades since have made the building one of the most impressive and beautiful structures in Savannah.

The church is open for visitors except during services, Monday through Saturday, 9:00 a.m. to 11:45 and 12:45 to 5:00 p.m., and it closed to visits on holy days such as Good Friday.

OTHER MONUMENTS OF INTEREST—CIVIL WAR AND RECONSTRUCTION

Three associated Confederate monuments can be found in Savannah, near to each other in Forsyth Park, a short walk south of the Forsyth Park Fountain. The largest of the monuments was put up in 1879, the figure of a proud, defeated soldier, shown wearing his tattered uniform. Cast in bronze, the oversize statue is on top of a forty-eight-foot shaft of marble and sandstone, which itself rests on a six-foot-high brick and earth terrace. This figure is one of the oldest and largest Confederate monuments in Georgia.

The busts of General Francis Stebbins Bartow and General Lafayette McLaws are next to the main Confederate Monument. Bartow

Confederate Monument.

was killed at the Battle of First Manassas (Bull Run) in 1861. McLaws lived on after the war, serving as president of the Confederate Veterans Association of Georgia until his death in 1898. These two busts were moved to the location from Chippewa Square in 1920 to make way for the Oglethorpe Monument to be erected there.

5 Age of Enterprise through World War I, 1877–1918

The four decades from the end of Reconstruction (1877) to the end of World War I (1918) saw the transition of the United States from a sorely divided nation with a war-ravaged southern section into a recognized world power. While the South, and Georgia in particular, had suffered greatly from the destruction of the Civil War, the nation's economy grew by leaps and bounds. The period saw the opening of the West, the completion of the transcontinental railroad, and the expansion of the rail network to remote areas of the nation. Shipping by river, rail, and sea brought new business opportunities, as crops, livestock, raw materials, and manufactured products, some of which had once only sold locally, now found national and international markets. Vast fortunes were made by entrepreneurs throughout the country in this "age of enterprise."

For Georgia and Savannah, the four decades following Reconstruction brought their own specific changes. White politicians, many of them former leaders of the Confederate regime, controlled Georgia politics. Through a variety of measures, ranging from "dirty tricks" like lost ballot boxes to violence such as lynching and cross burnings, black men were denied a political voice. Women, whether white or African American, did not have access to the vote in Georgia until the elections of 1922. Increasingly, public facilities like railroad cars, streetcars, theaters, hotels, and restaurants were strictly segregated along racial lines.

Like other states of the "New South," Georgia benefited from the great financial expansion of the era. The railroad network in the South, much of it destroyed during the Civil War, was rebuilt. The railroad shops, built a few years before the Civil War and expanded in this era, are now a major historical tourist attraction at the intersection of West Harris Street and Martin Luther King Boulevard.

Individual entrepreneurs in Savannah, some building on earlier fortunes, built grand homes and institutions that added to the already-rich architectural heritage of the city. Among the landmark structures of the era were the Telfair Academy (1875), the Savannah Cotton Exchange Building (1887), the Independent Presbyterian Church (rebuilt after the fire of 1889), and the Savannah City Hall (1905).

Although rice cultivation fell back with the end of slavery, cotton production continued to flourish. Cotton growers recognized a looming threat as the blight of the boll weevil spread from Texas eastward through these decades, finally reaching Georgia in 1916. Some new crops appeared, and Georgia peaches (which had been a minor state crop since the 1850s) became a nationally recognized crop by the 1870s and 1880s as rail transportation made

City Hall. The Savannah City Hall, with its gleaming dome, was erected at the intersection of Bull Street and Bay Street in 1905.

delivery of the fresh fruit to northern and western markets possible.

In 1898, the conflict with Spain and the short Spanish-American War reminded Carolinians how vulnerable they were to possible attack from the sea. The crumbling forts that had protected the port of Savannah from attack by sea were obviously of no use against the modern armored warships of the late nineteenth century, as the shattering of one brick wall at Fort Pulaski in April 1862 by Union bombardment had demonstrated. Hurriedly, new forts were planned and begun along the Gulf and Atlantic coasts. Savannah was reinforced with new concrete gun emplacements collectively known as Fort Screven on Tybee Island. None were

Georgia Peaches

Raphael Moses, from Columbus, Georgia, was one of the first to market peaches, shipping Georgia peaches out of state by rail in 1851, using champagne baskets. By 1858, a regular route for peach shipment ran by wagon to Augusta, thence by boat to Savannah, then by steamship to New York. Selective breeding of peaches yielded the Elberta peach, introduced by Samuel Henry Rumph in 1870 and named after his wife. The heart of the peach country was Fort Valley, about 190 miles west of Savannah. Peach County was established there in 1924.

completed before the war ended, but they remain today as reminders of that era.

Savannah introduced a system of horse-pulled street railroads in 1868, creating some controversies over the impact of rail transportation on the look of the city that would continue to plague local leaders in later years.

Arguments over whether the streetcars should detour around squares or cut straight through them foreshadowed later debates over the impact of highways and access ramps. The first electric streetcar line in Savannah was established in 1890.

With the advent of the automobile in the first decade of the twentieth century, the tension between advocates of preservation and advocates of commerce and modernity became even more heated, a dispute that would continue for the next century in one form or another.

Near the old City Market along Broughton Street, shops, stores, and (early in the twentieth century) movie theaters created a bustling shopping district that resembled the main streets of many small cities across the nation. Meanwhile, many of the grand homes of the antebellum period fell into disrepair, while a few new fortunes led to the building of additional mansions scattered through the Historic District. Some antebellum homes, such as the Wayne-Gordon House, were

beautifully maintained through the era, but dozens of others fell into disrepair or disuse, remaining in shabby condition through the period and well into the twentieth century.

South of Forsyth Park, developers built a new generation of homes, reflecting the architectural tastes of the Victorian era. Today a designated Victorian District, bounded by Martin Luther King Boulevard, East Broad Street, and Gwinnett and Anderson Streets, contains dozens of examples of the whimsical Victorian styles and features, such as elaborate gingerbread, rounded or octagonal porches and towers, stained-glass windows, second-floor balconies, turrets, and bay windows.

SITES

KING-TISDELL COTTAGE

514 East Huntington Street
(912) 234-8000

The small Victorian King-Tisdell Cottage, with elaborate gingerbread decoration on

King-Tisdell Cottage. This cottage represents the lifestyle of an African American family of the 1890s, and it is the starting point of the African American Heritage Trail.

the front porch, had originally been built on another site in 1896. When it was scheduled for demolition in 1970, the City of Savannah and the Historic Savannah Foundation purchased the building and moved it to its present location on East Huntington Street. The building is dedicated to preserving African American history and culture, and it is furnished with items typical of what might have been found in a late nineteenth-century African American home. Call ahead for hours and special exhibits or events.

GEORGIA STATE RAILROAD MUSEUM

655 Louisville Road
(912) 651-6823

A unique historical attraction in Savannah is the Georgia State Railroad Museum, next to the battlefield and near the Savannah History Museum. The museum offers a rare oppor-tunity to visit a rail repair shop reflecting the technologies used through the late nineteenth and early twentieth centuries at the height of the steam railroad era. The museum is the original site of the Central Savannah Railroad Repair Shops. The shops were built in the period 1851–1855 and included a distinctive roundhouse with a turntable for moving engines and tenders. Though the first facilities on the site date to that earlier period, they offer physical documentation of the age of enterprise when steam railroads tied the nation together after the Civil War and into the early twentieth century.

With the advent of diesel railroad engines, the shops fell into disuse, and the Savannah Repair Shops were closed in 1963. When the Southern Railway began demolishing some of the buildings on the property, concerned Savannah citizens worked to preserve the industrial site. The City of Savannah acquired

Railroad Museum roundhouse. The roundhouse at the Railroad Museum gives a unique view of the age of steam in railroading.

the property, and in 1989 the nonprofit Coastal Heritage Society took over management of the site.

Today the former Central Repair Shops are the largest and most complete railroad facility from the pre–Civil War period in the world. There are altogether twelve separate buildings or other structures open to visitors today. They include:

- **The Tender Frame Shop.** Originally built in 1855 to construct the frames for locomotive tenders, the building was expanded in 1899 to add a blueprint, drafting, and testing laboratory.
- **Machine Shop.** Completed in 1855, the building was severely damaged during Hurricane David in 1979.
- **Blacksmith Shop.** Also completed in 1855, this building contained thirteen forges and a steam hammer. Smoke from the forges was channeled through tunnels to the smokestack.
- **Smokestack.** Completed in 1855, this 125-foot brick chimney contained privies and showers around the base.
- **Engine House and Boiler Room.** This 1855 building contained a steam engine that provided power to belt-driven machinery throughout the site. The Finlay steam engine in this building is the oldest stationary steam engine made in Georgia known to survive in the United States.
- **Roundhouse and Turntable.** This distinctive structure and the engine turntable were at the heart of the site, and it was where locomotives were inspected and maintained. Half of the roundhouse was torn down in 1926 to accommodate larger steam engines of the era, accounting for the present shape of the structure.

Railroad Museum Smokestack. The smokestack at the Georgia State Railroad Museum vented the stationary engines at the repair shops, and it was encircled with workmen's privies.

Other facilities include the Coach Stop, Storehouse, Carpenter's Shop, Paint Shop, and Workers' Garden.

Specialized tours include visits to Executive Railcars, a tour of the "backshop" restoration area, steam power and handcar demonstrations, and visits to a model train room, set up by the Coastal Rail Buffs.

TELFAIR ACADEMY (AS MUSEUM, 1886)

121 Barnard Street (Telfair Square)
(912) 790-8800

The Telfair Academy at 121 Barnard Street is an art museum, located in a mansion built in 1818–1819 for Alexander Telfair. He was the son of Edward Telfair, who had served as governor of Georgia (1786–1787; 1790–1793). The building was designed by British architect William Jay and is a fine example of the Classical revival style of that period, reflecting Greek and Roman themes.

The mansion and other Telfair properties were inherited by Alexander's sister, Mary Telfair, who willed several structures to the city of Savannah. She stipulated that the mansion was to be an art museum, under the direction of Carl Ludwig Brandt, an internationally known German-born artist. Brandt served as director of the museum from 1883 (before it formally opened to the public in 1886), until his death in 1905.

To acquire exhibits, Brandt traveled to Europe with a sizable budget, visiting Munich, Vienna, Hamburg, Dusseldorf, and Paris. In Vienna, he commissioned five statues to be sculpted by Viktor Tilgner. They arrived and were installed in time for the opening of the museum in 1886. Today, those statues remain on display in front of the mansion, representing famous artists; left to right, they are Rubens, Raphael, Phidias, Michelangelo, and Rembrandt.

The west wing of the building, a former carriage house, was incorporated into the main structure in the 1880s. The interior has several unusually shaped rooms, including an octagonal drawing room and both a drawing room and a dining room with rounded ends. The museum now includes in its permanent collection many

Michelangelo. This statue of Michelangelo is one of five sculptures acquired by the Telfair Museum in 1884 and 1885, including Phidias, Rembrandt, Rubens, and Raphael. They have watched over Telfair Square for more than 130 years.

works by American artists, including George Bellows, Frederick Frieseke, and George Luks. The Telfair Academy now operates the modern Jepson Center, which also faces Telfair Square on the southwest side.

COTTON EXCHANGE BUILDING (1886)

The Cotton Exchange Building, at 100 East Bay Street, built in 1886, houses Savannah's Masonic lodge known as "Solomon's Lodge."

The building itself is constructed in the Romanesque style of the 1880s, designed by Francis Preston, a Boston architect, who was probably influenced by the leading Romanesque Revival architect, Henry Hobson Richardson. The red brick, iron window frames, copper finishing touches such as finials and copings, and rough exposed faces of the stone, known as "rustication," were all characteristic of the style that Richardson had made popular. The Cotton Exchange was constructed entirely over a public street, one of the first in the United States with such an arrangement.

In the front of the exchange, an iron fence with medallions representing authors and statesmen surrounds a statue of a winged lion and a fountain. The medallion fence at the Cotton Exchange had once been located at the Barclay-Wetter House, salvaged and moved to the Exchange Building when the house was demolished in 1950. Some of the same type of salvaged ironwork from the Barclay-Wetter House is found at the Philbrick-Eastman House at 17 West McDonough Street on Chippewa Square.

By the 1880s, when the Cotton Exchange was built, Savannah had become a long-established cotton export port. The Cotton Exchange served as a financial center

Cotton Exchange Building. The Cotton Exchange, with its statue of a winged lion, is a centerpiece of Factors Walk, facing on Bay Street since 1887.

for cotton brokers or factors, who had easy access to the cotton warehouses along Bay Street by way of Factors Walk.

The Savannah Masonic Lodge dates to 1734, the year following the founding of the Georgia colony. In 1735, the local Masonic lodge received its "warrant," or official status, from Britain. Oglethorpe himself was a Mason and the leader of the first lodge; the concern for the plight of the poor shown by Georgia's founders was a Masonic principle. The lodge took over the Cotton Exchange Building as its meeting place in 1972.

For these reasons, the building ties to several different eras of Savannah's history—the charitable goals of Oglethorpe and the other founders of Georgia as represented by the Masonic order, the reemergence of Savannah as a major financial center after the end of Reconstruction in the 1880s, and the dominance of cotton and the cotton trade in Savannah from well before the Civil War into the first two decades of the twentieth century.

THE WAVING GIRL STATUE

The statue of "The Waving Girl" evokes a famous and fond bit of Savannah history. Florence Martus, born in 1868, lived with her brother, George, the lighthouse keeper at the Elba Island Lighthouse. Beginning in 1887, at age nineteen, she began waving a handkerchief or lantern at passing ships. Sailors would return the greeting with a blast of a foghorn or a wave from the deck.

She kept up her waving for forty-four years until 1931, greeting some fifty thousand ships over her lifetime. A variety of legends and stories grew up about "the waving girl," who became known to sailors from all over the world. Some speculated that she had fallen in love with a sailor who had visited Savannah, while others thought she was simply lonely, living out on Elba Island. Her gesture had a

Waving Girl Statue. The legend of Florence Martus, who greeted ships arriving at Savannah from 1887 to 1931, is kept alive by this statue facing the river.

deep emotional appeal for sailors who had left wives and sweethearts behind.

After she retired, her story lived on, although she denied the rumors of a lost love and simply said she wanted to welcome ships to Savannah. She passed away in 1934; during World War II, a Liberty ship was named for her. The SS *Florence Martus* was christened in 1943. In 1972, the City of Savannah commissioned the statue that stands at the eastern end of River Street, in Morrell Park on the Savannah waterfront, sculpted by Felix de Weldon. He was already famous for the Iwo Jima Memorial in Arlington, Virginia. The statue of Florence Martus still welcomes visitors to Savannah.

BONAVENTURE CEMETERY AND LITTLE GRACIE (1889)

330 Bonaventure Road
(912) 651-6843

There is no charge for admission to the Bonaventure Cemetery, which is open 8:00 a.m. to 5:00 p.m. daily. At the cemetery office, with the entrance located around the back of the gatehouse, visitors can obtain a map and directions to particular graves or points of interest.

The cemetery dates back to a private grave-yard on a plantation owned by John Mulryne. The cemetery was opened to nonfamily members in 1868 and was purchased by

Bonaventure Cemetery gate. The Bonaventure Cemetery, first established before the Civil War, was acquired by the City of Savannah in 1907.

Among the most well-known sculptures once located in Bonaventure was *The Bird Girl*, famously photographed by Jack Leigh for the book cover of Berendt's book. That statue, since removed, is now on display in the Jepson Center.

Another well-known statue is that of "Gracie," located on a small plot in the "E" section of the cemetery. These and many other sculptures combine with the gently moving Spanish moss hanging from the oak trees to create a haunted ambience.

The story of the statue of Gracie Watson, a six-year-old girl, is part of the cemetery's lore. "Little Gracie," as she is remembered, was

Gracie. Among the many legends associated with the Bonaventure Cemetery is that of Gracie Watkins, who died as child in 1889. Her statue and grave plot are now protected with an iron fence.

Bird Girl replica statue. Made famous from the book cover photograph by John Leigh for John Berendt's *Midnight in the Garden of Good and Evil*, the original statue of the "Bird Girl" was moved to the Jepson Center, and this replica is found in the Savannah History Museum.

the City of Savannah in 1907. The cemetery was made nationally famous by naturalist John Muir, who stayed in it overnight before launching a "one-thousand-mile walk to the Gulf" in 1916. In more recent years, Bonaventure Cemetery played a part in the 1994 nonfiction novel *Midnight in the Garden of Good and Evil* by John Berendt.

born in 1883 to W. J. and Frances Watson. Her parents were from Boston and had moved to Savannah to manage the luxurious Pulaski Hotel. The little girl was the darling of the hotel, but just before her sixth birthday she died from pneumonia. Her heartbroken parents had her interred at Bonaventure, and a sculpture for her grave marker, based on photographs of her, was installed on the grave. Soon after her death, her parents moved back to New England. The poignant statue soon caught the imagination of visitors to Bonaventure, who took pity on the lonely girl. It became a tradition in Savannah for children to bring small gifts of candy or other presents and place them on the grave. Over the years, legends of sightings of the ghost of Gracie playing near the site of the Pulaski Hotel, and the legend of her lonely statue in Bonaventure Cemetery, grew. Eventually, contributors collected money to put a small fence around the grave plot to protect the statue and the grave site from foot traffic and vandalism.

INDEPENDENT PRESBYTERIAN CHURCH (REBUILT 1891)

Bull Street and Oglethorpe Avenue

This striking Presbyterian church is one of the oldest in Savannah, tracing its origins to 1755, when the congregation was first established in a building facing what is now Ellis Square. The church is regarded as the "mother church" of all Presbyterian congregations in Georgia. John Joachim Zubly, a member of the Continental Congress, was the first minister.

The original building, which had been used by the British as a stable and powder-storage magazine during the American War for Independence, burned down in 1790. Materials were recovered from that ruin to construct a wall on West Hull Street, across from the

Independent Presbyterian Church. The Presbyterian Church of Savannah can trace its origins to the colonial period, but the present church was finished in 1891 after damage from an 1889 fire.

present-day church. A second Presbyterian church structure, built on Telfair Square in 1800, was damaged by a hurricane. A third church was erected on the present site, finished in 1819. The structure of the third building was so elegant that it drew national recognition. Its dedication was attended by national figures, including President James Monroe and John C. Calhoun.

During the 1820s the organist of the church was Lowell Mason, who composed the music for many hymns still sung today, including "Nearer My God to Thee" and "Joy to the

World." Mason also founded the first Sunday school for black children in the United States, set up for the First Bryan Baptist Church. Mason moved on to Boston and later to New York City as one of the leaders of church music in the United States.

Woodrow Wilson (U.S. president, 1913–1921) married his first wife, who was born in Savannah, in the church in 1885. She was Ellen Louise Axson, and the marriage ceremony was conducted jointly by her grandfather, L. S. K. Axson, and by Wilson's father, who were both Presbyterian ministers. Reverend L. S. K. Axson served as minister of the church from 1857 through 1886. A replica of the manse parlor of Reverend Axson is found in the present-day Axson Memorial Building, built in 1928.

Although the church had survived the Civil War intact, as did most of Savannah, it was destroyed in a great city fire of 1889. Some of the original marble fixtures, such as the baptismal font, were rescued, and the congregation decided to rebuild the church as an exact replica of the 1819 structure.

Some observers have ranked this church as the most impressive structure in Savannah.

SPANISH-AMERICAN WAR MEMORIAL (WAR 1898; STATUE 1931)

Forsyth Park, south end of park facing Park Avenue and looking south down Bull Street

During the Spanish-American War of 1898, Savannah was one of the major ports for embarkation of troops to fight in Cuba. The war sprang out of American popular sentiment against the cruelties of Spanish repression of Cuban revolutionaries who sought independence from Spain. As a result of the short war (April–August 1898), the

Spanish-American War Monument. Known as "The Hiker," this statue was erected in honor of Georgia veterans of the 1898 Spanish-American War.

United States gained the territories of Puerto Rico and Guam from Spain and secured a lease on forty-five-square-mile Guantanamo Bay as a naval base, while Cuba won its independence from Spain. Spain ceded the Philippine Islands to the United States, and the United States governed the Philippines as a territory until the conquest of the islands by Japan in World War II and then their full independence as a republic in 1946. The Spanish-American War is the event that marked the emergence of the United States as a world military power.

In 1931, this large bronze statue was mounted on a stone pedestal to honor soldiers from Georgia who fought in the brief 1898 war. Although representing soldiers from across Georgia, the statue was placed in Savannah because it sent more men to the Spanish-American War than any other

Georgia city. Georgia troops who served in the war made up the Third Georgia Regiment that included Company K, made up of about fifty men from Savannah. Each of the four sides of the base contains a metal plaque listing specific Georgia veterans of the war.

The statue is known as "The Hiker," from the term that Spanish-American War veterans used to describe themselves, after hiking miles across country in Cuba and the Philippines. The Hiker carries a Krag-Jorgensen rifle, standard issue in the U.S. Army from about 1895 through 1903. The Hiker statue was first sculpted by Theodora Alice Ruggles Kitson (1871–1932). A prolific and talented sculptor, she created numerous war memorial statues; the Hiker is her most famous, first shown in 1906 at the University of Minnesota. The model for the figure was an actual veteran of the Spanish-American War, Leonard Sefing Jr. of Allentown, Pennsylvania, chosen for the role after a national competition. At least fifty bronze castings of the sculpture were placed around the United States. Fittingly, the statue in Forsyth Park faces south, as if defending Savannah from a Spanish attack, echoing the placement of the statue of Oglethorpe.

FORT SCREVEN (1897–1901)
(912) 786-5444 for hours and fees

The history of Fort Screven can be experienced with a visit to the Tybee Island Museum. It is reached via Highway 80 east from Savannah to Tybee Island. On the island, turn left at the stop light onto Campbell Avenue and follow to the end and turn left on Van Horne Avenue; then take the first (right) on Meddin Drive. The museum is in Battery Garland at 30 Meddin Drive. Tickets to the museum are sold at the Tybee Island Lighthouse directly across from the Battery Garland Museum.

Battery Garland. Erected as part of the defenses of Savannah, Battery Garland at Fort Screven on Tybee Island was typical of the Endicott System of coastal forts built in the 1890s and early 1900s.

Although defenders of Savannah from the earliest days of the settlement under George Oglethorpe realized that the mouth of the Savannah River on the Atlantic Ocean was a natural point for coastal defense works, an actual fort was not constructed at the spot until the 1890s. As early as 1786, the Georgia legislature had authorized a fort, to be named Fort Screven in honor of James Screven, a hero of the Revolution, to be built on the spot. During the Civil War, Union gun emplacements on Tybee Island included the rifled guns that breached the walls of Fort Pulaski. By 1875, the Army Corps of Engineers acquired land on Tybee Island for the construction of a permanent fort to defend the river access to Savannah.

In 1885, President Grover Cleveland set up a joint army, navy, and civilian board that was chaired by Secretary of War William Crowninshield Endicott. The plan of fortifications planned by the Endicott Board took into account development of ship armor, advances in shipboard and shore weaponry, and the need for a coastal defense system. As part of the Endicott System, a number of modern (by late nineteenth-century standards) forts were built along the nation's coasts, using concrete, with heavy guns often concealed from direct observation from the sea behind sand dunes and plantings. The emplacements on Tybee Island were the result of the Endicott recommendations and reflected many elements of the new approach.

The first of the seven batteries that made up Fort Screven was started in 1897 and was completed in July 1898, just before the end of the Spanish-American War. Over the period 1898–1904, a total of six more gun batteries were installed nearby. Like other forts of the Endicott System up and down the East Coast of the United States, Fort Screven never came under fire from an enemy and never fired its weapons against enemy ships—only in practice.

Informally known as "Fort Tybee," the army named the seven separate gun batteries Fort Screven after the name originally approved by the Georgia legislature more than a century earlier. Of the seven gun batteries, Battery Hambright (near Fort Pulaski) and Battery Garland, with its museum, are now open for visitors. Remains of the other batteries—Brumby, Habersham, Fenwick, Backus, and Gantt—can still be viewed but are not open to visit.

Battery Hambright is open for visiting at no charge near Fort Pulaski. Like other batteries of Fort Screven, it was planned in anticipation of the Spanish-American War but not completed until 1901, more than two years after the war was over.

THE GINGERBREAD HOUSE (1899)

1921 Bull Street (Bull Street and Thirty-Sixth Street)
(912) 358-8440

The Gingerbread House was built in 1899 and occupied by Cord and Bernardine Asendorf and their children. Cord Asendorf, born in 1858, had immigrated to Savannah from Germany in 1872 and worked in his uncle's grocery business at Jones and Habersham Streets. By 1879, at age twenty-one, he was operating his own grocery on Tattnall Street. In 1885, he opened a larger grocery at East Broad and Liberty Streets. After marrying Bernadine in 1890, he engaged the Hawley Construction Company to build the Gingerbread House. According to tax records, the house cost $3,000.

After retiring from the grocery business on the completion of his house, Cord Asendorf remained active, managing a number of Savannah properties until his death in 1944.

The Gingerbread House is Savannah's prime example of "Steamboat Gothic" Victorian architecture.

Over the years, the house earned a national reputation as a landmark, and famous visitors included President Franklin Roosevelt, during a tour of Savannah in November 1933.

Today the well-preserved house is regarded as a leading Savannah landmark of the Victorian "Steamboat Gothic" style, with elaborate wood exterior decoration, and it is operated as a wedding venue. The interior of the Gingerbread House features a conservatory, three fireplaces, a wooden staircase,

and Victorian-era furnishings. The private courtyard has a gazebo and a waterfall.

WAYNE-GORDON HOUSE AND ANDREW LOW HOUSE (FOUNDATION OF GIRL SCOUTS, 1912)

For tour hours and fees, call (912) 233-4501

There are three sites near each other that relate to Juliette Gordon Low, the founder of the American Girl Scouts. Her birthplace is the "Wayne-Gordon House" at 10 East Oglethorpe

Wayne-Gordon House. This home on the corner of Bull and Oglethorpe Streets was the birthplace of Juliette Gordon Low, the founder of the American Girl Scouts.

Avenue, on the corner of Bull Street. Two other properties are part of the "Juliette Gordon Low Historic District": the Andrew Low House at 329 Abercorn Street and the carriage house behind it.

Today the Girl Scouts of America own her birthplace, the Wayne-Gordon House, and the building serves as both a historic house museum and a national center for the American Girl Scout movement. The house itself dates back to the period 1818–1821,

when it was originally built for the mayor of Savannah, James Moore Wayne.

In 1911, Juliette Gordon Low met Robert Baden Powell, founder of the Boy Scouts, and she began working with an organization known as the "Girl Guides." Staying in the Gordon ancestral home in Savannah, she began the Girl Scout movement in 1912, recruiting members locally and having them meet at the home and in the carriage house. In 1953, the American Girl Scouts organization purchased the home and opened it with period furnishings in 1956.

Both the Andrew Low House and the Wayne-Gordon House are excellent showcases for the lifestyle of wealthy families in Savannah in the antebellum and later periods. The architecture, contents, and gardens of the three buildings convey the lifestyle of the wealthiest Savannah families in the early to late nineteenth century.

The large rooms of the Andrew Low House feature plaster cornices and carved woodwork. The elegance continues outside, with a brick-walled garden in the rear of the home and a front garden with two hourglass-shaped flower beds.

The Wayne-Gordon House originally resembled many other Savannah single and double houses built in the decades from the early national period until after the Civil War. Many simple houses from the period had similar floor plans and were known as "Savannah boxes." However, in this house the owners expanded the floor plan and added elegant details, which included two curved bays at the rear, stucco facing that resembled stone blocks on the exterior, arch treatments of second-floor windows, and a formal front portico with columns.

Andrew Low House. Built by the richest cotton factor in Savannah, Andrew Low II, the father-in-law of Juliette Gordon Low, this home is one of Savannah's finest house museums.

OTHER MONUMENTS OF INTEREST—AGE OF ENTERPRISE

GORDON MONUMENT

In the center of Wright Square is a monument to William Washington Gordon, erected in 1883. Gordon was the founder of the Central Railroad. The monument was erected in 1883, by his son, W. W. Gordon Jr., who represented those in the company who continued to insist that the company remain independent. To make way for the monument, the grave of Tomochichi was moved to the southeast corner of the square where the Tomochichi Monument, in the form of a boulder, now sits.

THE COHEN HUMANE FOUNTAIN

Located in the median of Victory Drive at Bull Street, this fountain replaced one that had originally been set up at another intersection in 1880, with a unique function. The original "humane" fountain had been located at Broad and St. Julian Streets, on a line between the Central Railroad Depot and the port, and had been set up so that horses and mules hauling wagons along that route between the rail station and the docks could stop for water. The Cohen Fountain that replaced it in 1933 was established with funds from the estate of Percival Randolph Cohen, and it was designed by architect Henrik Wallin. The fountain spills into an octagonal pool that is about twelve feet across and a foot deep. As mules and horses gave way to trucks, the original purpose was lost, and in 1933 the fountain was moved to the intersection of Bay and Whitaker Streets. Two more moves, in 1945 and another in 1960, brought the "Humane" Fountain to its present location. It serves as a reminder of an almost forgotten era in which the heavy cargos of freight were shifted from the rails to the port by animal power, engaging the kindness and sympathy of Savannah citizens.

MYERS "CANINE DRINKING FOUNTAIN"

The Myers "Canine Drinking Fountain" is a replica of an 1897 fountain originally located in Forsyth Park, funded by former mayor Herman Myers. Now located in Troupe Square, it has become known as a canine drinking fountain because its low drip basins are just the right height for dogs from the neighborhood.

BISHOP TURNER MONUMENT (HENRY McNEIL TURNER)

The Bishop Turner Monument, a five-by-six-foot granite slab with a cast aluminum plaque set in it, is located on the northeast side of the intersection of Fahm and Turner Streets. Henry McNeal Turner (1834–1919) was a bishop of the African Methodist Episcopal Church and a nationally known figure in the 1880s and 1890s, particularly for his advocacy of black emigration from the United States to Liberia in West Africa. He had served briefly in the Georgia legislature during Reconstruction and was responsible for establishing many AME churches throughout the state.

During the midyears of the twentieth century, Savannah, like many cities in the United States, faced a series of crises and profound changes. Transportation was revolutionized with new technologies. Automobile and air travel supplemented rail travel as the means for tourists and business travelers to get to and around the city. Streetcars were gradually replaced with bus lines, and in the 1950s diesel-powered trains replaced coal and steam power.

Like other American cities, Savannah grew with the coming of the automobile, with suburbs and, later, shopping malls expanding to the south. Airports, some formerly used by the military, opened to passenger aircraft and general (that is, private) aircraft. The interstate highway system, begun in the 1950s, helped facilitate the arrival of tourists.

Ocean transport also modernized, with the development of oil supertankers and, later, huge container ships and ocean cruise ships; the port of Savannah adapted to the new, massive ships.

While such technological changes impacted Savannah, the city also went through the

Container ship. Huge container ships like the *NYK Meteor* now regularly call at the port of Savannah.

Preservation and Restoration

Continuing a conflict that had begun to surface in the late nineteenth century, the struggle between progress and preservation emerged as a major local issue in Savannah. Since the city had escaped the destruction of the Civil War, and since it contained hundreds of homes, churches, and commercial buildings from the early nineteenth century, it was an ideal setting for the national focus on restoration and preservation that began slowly in the 1920s and then blossomed in the 1950s and 1960s.

The forces of preservation and commerce clashed over issues such as the development of business neighborhoods, and the destruction of two squares on Montgomery Street (Liberty Square, at the intersection of Montgomery and West President Streets, and Elbert Square, on Montgomery between Turner and Perry) to facilitate access to the city's business districts from Highway 17, by the 1970s. Today, tree plantings along Montgomery Street at the two intersections show where the former squares were obliterated.

By the 1960s civic leaders had come to recognize that a major modern asset of the city was its rich historical architectural heritage, as well as its many existing monuments and public sculptures. For this reason, many of the major nineteenth-century buildings in Savannah now open as house museums are a product of the late twentieth century nationwide and local focus on historic preservation.

major wars of the midcentury: World War II (1941–1945), the Korean War (1950–1953), and the Vietnam War (1968–1975). Savannah felt the impact of each of these wars as local men and women went off to serve in the nation's armed forces.

For African American residents of Savannah, the decades from the 1940s through the 1970s were a period of profound change. The nationwide civil rights revolution produced, first the *Brown v. Topeka* court decision that required the integration of public schools in 1954. By 1964 and 1965, the Civil Rights Acts brought racial integration to public transportation, public accommodation (such as restaurants and theaters), and housing. Local leaders like the Reverend Ralph Gilbert worked with national leaders to bring the changes to Savannah, heralded with the hiring of the city's first black policeman in 1946. Several museums devoted to African American culture and heritage can be visited today as reminders of the effort to achieve equal rights and to recognize the rich heritage of African Americans in the United States and the South.

Tourism, largely suspended during World War II, was given a boost in the post–World War II years, as out-of-state visitors discovered the unique historical ambience of southern cities like Charleston, Savannah, and St. Augustine.

SITES

OLD CITY MARKET AND JOHNNY MERCER STATUE

Today a shopping, restaurant, and arts neighborhood occupies the ground where the Savannah City Market once stood. Earlier structures on the site were built in 1788, 1820, and 1872. The Market Structure built in 1872 was an elaborate brick building with Romanesque arches and large circular windows. In 1954, that building was torn down.

Rehabilitation of the four-block area began in 1985, with a centerpiece being a nineteen-thousand-square-foot Art Center with low-cost artists' studios. With that facility

Horses and wagon. The horses Jeb (left) and Murphy (right) patiently wait as passengers load aboard their tour wagon at the City Market.

was unveiled in November 2009. Cofounder of Capitol Records, Mercer wrote more than fifteen hundred songs, including such all-time hits as "Moon River," "One for My Baby," "On the Atchison, Topeka and the Santa Fe," "That Old Black Magic," and "Summer Wind." Many of his songs became favorites of singers like Frank Sinatra and Hoagy Carmichael. Mercer won four Oscars for Best Song, along with many other awards.

Johnny Mercer Statue. The statue of songwriter Johnny Mercer is found at the east end of the City Market, leaning on a fire hydrant.

as an anchor, the surrounding neighborhood soon flourished with small shops, restaurants, and an active nightlife. Located between Franklin and Ellis Squares, several of the nightclubs in the market area feature live music every evening.

Appropriately enough, a life-size statue of Savannah-born songwriter Johnny Mercer (1909–1976) is found casually leaning against a fire hydrant, reading a newspaper, at the Ellis Square end of the City Market area. Sculpted by Susie Chisholm, the statue

Prohibition in Georgia and National Prohibition

Long before national *Prohibition of the sale of alcohol went into effect in 1920, Georgia and Savannah had a preview of the conditions the law would create. In 1907, Prohibitionists in the state legislature voted in statewide prohibition in Georgia.*

The enforcement of the law would require the cooperation of local authorities. Resistance to the idea of alcohol prohibition was so strong in Savannah that a movement was started to have Chatham County secede from Georgia and form its own state. That proved unnecessary, as the local police and mayor's office simply ignored the law. At least four hundred, and by one estimate as many as seven hundred, shops continued to sell liquor in Savannah in defiance of the 1907 law. Bars known as "blind tigers" proliferated. They were so called because of a legend that a customer could pay to see a "blind tiger" through a peephole and would then be treated to a "free" drink. The term soon applied to speakeasies of all sorts that operated openly as saloons.

Of the four hundred blind tigers reported in business in Savannah in 1913, Prohibitionists succeeded in closing only four.

The city was able to get revenue out of tolerating the speakeasies. Plainclothes police detectives would target one hundred blind tigers on a single day with a summons. Each owner summoned would go to the chief of police and post a $100 bond; however, when the case was called before a judge, no one would show up, and the proprietors would forfeit the bond, providing a steady and reliable source of city income. So, when nationwide Prohibition went into effect in 1920, Savannah had already developed a host of methods of evading the law, including blind tigers, rumrunners, and secret corn-liquor stills.

No doubt, the fact that cities like Savannah, Charleston, New Orleans, and other southern cities developed reputations as "centers of sin" was due to the fact that, unlike the rural counties in the South that controlled the state legislatures, these urban pockets strongly and successfully opposed Prohibition and developed reputations for scoffing at unpopular laws.

Prohibition Museum car. This Model A coupe, fitted out as a rumrunner car, is parked in the City Market Square; a load of corn liquor can be spotted in the rumble seat.

IMINAL LINE-UP
MACHINE GUN
JACK McGURN
AL CAPONE

Costumed interpreter Marcia Palmer poses with 1920s gangsters at the Prohibition Museum.

PROHIBITION MUSEUM

209 West Julian Street
(912) 220-1249

A modern attraction facing the City Market is Savannah's Prohibition Museum. This extensive museum offers a vast collection of artifacts and displays from the Prohibition era in the United States, with costumed interpreters offering short presentations on different aspects of the movement to ban alcohol and answering questions about the displays.

In addition to discussing Prohibition in Georgia and Savannah, the museum offers a thorough history of the nineteenth-century temperance movement, with interactive displays showing the positions of both "dries" and "wets"—that is, Prohibitionists and anti-Prohibitionists—as well as coverage of national Prohibition from 1920 to 1934.

With its range of coverage, the museum speaks to both late nineteenth-century developments and events of the early to mid-twentieth century. Displays cover a wide variety of topics, including the growth of organized crime and the influence of bootlegger car drivers on the evolution of NASCAR racing.

A unique feature of the museum is a fully stocked bar in "speakeasy" style; it may be the only museum in the United States where visitors (those over twenty-one, of course) can order a drink of their choice.

FLANNERY O'CONNOR CHILDHOOD HOME (MEMORIALIZING CAREER, 1950s–1960s)

207 East Charlton Street
(912) 233-6014

Flannery O'Connor (Mary Flannery O'Connor) was born and raised until the age of thirteen in a small home, now a house museum dedicated to her work and to literary meetings. She suffered from lupus and died at age thirty-nine in 1964. The house itself is a modest example of the Greek Revival style, originally built in 1856.

Over O'Connor's short life, she gained national and international fame for her works of fiction, including two novels and numerous short stories, as well as essays and lectures. With a perspective as a southern Catholic, her fiction featured characters who were usually economically poor and spiritually troubled. Her works won wide admiration from contemporary critics, who praised what they called her "dark humor" and her evocation of the South in language and setting. Some compared her work to that of writers in the earlier Southern Renaissance (usually associated with the 1920s and 1930s), such as William Faulkner and Tennessee Williams, while others found

World War II Monument. The "Cracked Earth" Monument to Savannah-area soldiers killed in World War II is in Rousakis Plaza on the waterfront.

her Catholic perspective on life in the South distinct and unique. Numerous critics and commentators identified her perspective as "southern Gothic."

Her two novels were *Wise Blood* (1952) and *The Violent Bear It Away* (1960). In addition, she published numerous short stories and a collection of essays titled *A Good Man Is Hard to Find* (1955). Works published after her death in 1964 included three collections: *Everything That Rises Must Converge* (1965), *Mystery and Manners* (1969), and *Collected Stories* (1974).

WORLD WAR II "CRACKED EARTH" MONUMENT

Located on West River Street, across from Whitaker Street, is this monument to Savannah-area servicemen and -women killed in World War II, 1941–1945. The striking monument is officially known as "The World Apart," and more informally, as the "Cracked Earth" Monument.

Originally planned to be installed in Oglethorpe Square, with the military associations of Oglethorpe, objections to that site were raised because the modern/contemporary design and scale of the proposed sculpture (more than twenty-nine feet high) did not seem to fit into the context of the historic homes around Oglethorpe Square.

The present site on River Street was selected as more appropriate because of the contemporary and modern look of the area, its wider and more open space, and the flow of tourist traffic. Furthermore, the riverfront had associations with World War II shipbuilding. The Veterans Council set a fund-raising goal of $1 million. After agreeing on the final site in 2006, the council selected a team including architect Eric Meyerhoff and local sculptors Susie Chisholm and Garland Weeks, who produced the first design. The team came up with the split-earth design, but it also planned some accompanying statues that were not included in the final choice.

The monument is a large globe of the earth, split into two halves, representing the world divided by war. A walkway goes through the two halves, and the names of 527 men who died in the war who came from Savannah and surrounding Chatham County are listed on the walls facing the interior walkway. A surrounding bench is adorned with medallions for the army, navy, marines, army air corps, coast guard, and merchant marines.

NATIONAL MUSEUM OF THE MIGHTY EIGHTH AIR FORCE (1941–1945)

175 Bourne Avenue, Pooler, GA 31322
(exit 102 from Interstate 95)
Open daily, 9:00 a.m. to 5:00 p.m.
(912) 748-8888

This museum is dedicated to the Eighth Air Force, the main bombing force of the United States Army Air Force in Europe during World War II. Galleries and exhibits include documents, artifacts, illustrations, and interactive exhibits, presenting the following aspects of the story:

Prelude to WWII. This exhibit documents the events that led up to the war.

Mission Experience. Three short movies that begin every half hour show the experience of a member of an air crew,

This B-47 Stratojet at the Mighty Eighth Air Force Museum faces busy Interstate 95 in nearby Pooler, Georgia.

flying a bombing mission from England during World War II.

Combat Gallery. This exhibit includes complete aircraft such as a B-17, bombs on display, partial aircraft sections, and aircraft models, as well as dioramas depicting the Ploesti raid and the transformation of a British farm into an airfield.

Airman Down. Visitors enter through an unfurled parachute to exhibits that show a safe house where downed airmen hid from capture, as well as artifacts from POW camps where captured airmen were interned during the war.

Lights Come On Again. This exhibit focuses on "V-E Day," May 8, 1945, when Germany surrendered.

Honoring the 8th. Exhibits here include some of the many heroes of the Eighth Air Force and a film documenting the contributions of the Eighth Air Force to the war.

Airmen Memorial. This exhibit is dedicated to the twenty-six thousand members of the Eighth Air Force who lost their lives in World War II.

Modern 8th Air Force. This gallery tells the tale of the Eighth Air Force in the decades since World War II, including its present role.

Other exhibits. Other exhibits give the stories of individual heroes, showcase works of art related to the Eighth Air Force, and include the full-scale aircraft display on the grounds of the museum. These include an F-4C Phantom and a Soviet Mikoyan-Gurevich 17A, or "MiG." A B-47 Stratojet is on display behind the museum near the Memorial Gardens, on loan from the National Museum of the United States Air Force in Dayton, Ohio. The bomber is a striking monument itself, quite visible from the busy Interstate 95.

MRS. WILKES' BOARDINGHOUSE (1943–PRESENT)

A Savannah institution since 1943 is a "boardinghouse" at 107 Jones Street. At that location, Mrs. Dennis Dixon owned a boardinghouse and asked Sema Wilkes to help out. Sema Wilkes had joined her husband in Savannah, where he worked for the railroad when their farmland near Vidalia, Georgia, was taken over for an air force base during World War II.

After working for Mrs. Dixon, Sema Wilkes and her husband Lois H. Wilkes bought the two side-by-side residences at 105 and 107 West Jones Street on November 24, 1965, from historic Savannah, as part of a planned restoration project around Pulaski Square. Through the 1970s and 1980s, the fame of Mrs. Wilkes' cooking slowly spread, with numerous newspaper and magazine articles drawing attention to the home-style cooking

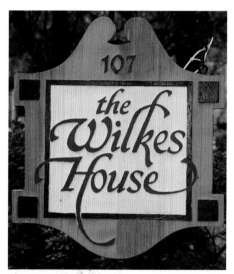

Mrs. Wilkes' sign. One of the most historic and popular restaurants in Savannah is marked by this tiny, modest sign.

and service, as well as the low prices, which gradually climbed from 75 cents to $5 a meal over those decades. Testimonials by well-known celebrities such as newscaster David Brinkley and actors Lorne Greene and Richard Chamberlain added to the word-of-mouth reputation of the dining room.

Customers would line up outside, often for the length of a block, and at 11:30 they would enter and sit down at five or six group tables, each seating eight to ten customers, where southern home cooking was served family-style. With articles in *Time*, *Redbook*, and *Esquire*, the economical meals attracted national and international attention. Mrs. Wilkes never advertised the restaurant, nor did a sign outside proclaim the location until 1987, when she finally allowed the small sign announcing the location. A cookbook with many of Mrs. Wilkes' recipes has sold more than one hundred thousand copies. Today Marcia Thompson, Sema Wilkes' granddaughter, carries on the tradition of home cooking and family-style dining.

SAVANNAH THEATRE (1948 RESTORATION)

222 Bull Street
(912) 233-7764

Located on the northeast corner of Chippewa Square, the Savannah Theatre is the oldest continually operating theater in the United States, first opened on the same spot in 1818. Due to fires and storm damage, the building has undergone two major renovations following fires in 1906 and 1948. The 1948 remodel into a motion picture theater that opened in 1950 resulted in the present-day art deco or "art moderne" look.

The original structure was designed by architect William Jay, who also designed the Telfair Mansion (now the Telfair Academy on

Savannah Theatre. The 1940s look of the Savannah Theatre belies its two-century history.

Telfair Square) and the Owens-Thomas House on Oglethorpe Square. The modern façade from the late 1940s leaves the impression that the structure is a relatively new one, despite its two-hundred-year existence on the same spot.

Over the two centuries of the Savannah Theatre's history, many internationally known actors performed there, including Edwin Booth, Oscar Wilde, Sarah Bernhardt, W. C. Fields, Tyrone Power, and Lillian Russell. Today the theater hosts live performances including local and touring musical shows. Check by phone or newspaper listings for details of currently scheduled performances and ticket prices.

WEBB MILITARY MUSEUM (WORLD WAR II, 1941–1945, AND MORE RECENT WARS)

411 East York Street
(912) 663-0398

The Webb Military Museum is another unique museum of Savannah. Founded by Gary Webb, the museum represents a lifetime of collecting. Webb was inspired by stories from his mother, Doreen Webb. Doreen, born in 1927, had lived through the "blitz" of London and had relatives in Germany. Gary (himself raised in military bases around the world) began collecting artifacts of World War II as a child.

Among the artifacts are uniforms and equipment from America's wars, with special emphasis on World War II and the Vietnam War, although there are artifacts from all of America's major conflicts.

The collection includes uniforms, medals, photographs, weapons, documents, helmets, flags, autographed items, diaries, newspapers and magazines, maps, and even a portion of a Russian MiG aircraft. Among the unique aspects of this museum is that Gary Webb can tell you not only the story of each item in the museum, how it fits into the larger story of the war in which it played a part, and how it relates to other items in the displays but also exactly how and when he acquired it. His enthusiasm for the collection and each artifact is infectious, and visitors, including children, come away with a store of details about American military history that cannot be gained in any other way.

Bob Hope shirt. The Webb Military Museum displays a wide variety of memorabilia, including this shirt worn by Bob Hope during his performances for U.S. troops in Vietnam.

DAVENPORT HOUSE (OPENED AS MUSEUM 1963)

324 East State Street
(912) 236-8097

The citywide debate over preservation of the Isaiah Davenport House on Columbia Square in the 1950s is regarded as the initiation of the modern preservation movement in Savannah.

The house had been built by a successful artisan, Isaiah Davenport, and on his death in 1827, his widow, Sarah Clark Davenport, continued to live in the building and manage

Davenport House. The restoration of this building marked the beginning of the modern restoration and preservation movement in Savannah.

it as a boardinghouse. In 1840, she sold the home to the Baynard family, and it remained in that family until 1949. By that time the whole neighborhood had become run down, and the house was simply a shabby rooming house. In the 1930s, the Historic American Buildings Survey had identified the building as architecturally significant. A group of concerned Savannah citizens banded together in the 1950s to purchase and preserve the building, the first action of the Historic Savannah Foundation. After careful restoration, the building became the foundation's headquarters in 1955, and in 1963 the first floor was opened as a

museum. In later years, the upper floors were also opened to the public, and the foundation undertook more meticulous restoration to early nineteenth-century decor, with wallpaper and furnishings that reflected the styles of the 1820s. This building launched the Savannah restoration and preservation effort that later saved hundreds of buildings through a system of a revolving loan fund and grants.

The house is as much a monument to the modern preservation movement as it is a monument to the antebellum period in which it was first built.

OTHER MONUMENTS OF INTEREST—MID-TWENTIETH CENTURY

POLICE OFFICERS MONUMENT

Located in the median of Oglethorpe Avenue at Habersham Street, across from the city police headquarters, is a statue that is a memorial to Savannah police officers who died in the line of duty. The granite base was set up in 1964, and the statue finally installed in 1982. City patrolman R. I. Ketterman was used as the model for the statue.

The base is inscribed with this simple message: "Above and Beyond / Lest We Forget."

Listed on the base are the names of police officers killed in the line of duty from 1869 to the present.

The origin of the monument is owed to the Police Officers' Wives Association. The group had formed a committee in 1963, spurred on by the murder of Patrolman Harry H. Akins. The committee was dedicated to researching the names of those who had died in the line of duty and worked to establish a monument in their honor, with the granite base installed the following year.

Police Officers Monument. This monument near the police station is dedicated to Savannah's fallen law officers.

Marine Monument. The small stone monument to the United States Marines is found at the intersection of Bull and Gwinnett Streets, at the northern end of Forsyth Park.

MARINE MONUMENT

The Marine Monument on Bull Street at the Gaston Street entrance to Forsyth Park was erected in 1947 to honor those U.S. Marines from Chatham County lost in World War II. It is a piece of white Georgia marble with bronze plaques.

MONUMENT TO CHATHAM COUNTY MARINERS

In 1974, a monument on River Street across from Abercorn Street was set up to honor mariners from Chatham County who were lost at sea. It is in the form of an anchor and chain set on a rectangular base made up of four marble slabs in a shallow brick pool.

Over the recent decades, Savannah, like many other older cities in the United States, has worked to preserve and to capitalize on its rich history. Such efforts have ranged from very serious and historically accurate preservation and restoration of older buildings, and the establishment of professionally run museums, to more commercial activities, such as shops, bars, and restaurants that evoke historical origins, to specialized tours and guides and to commercial souvenir shops.

Businesses, including restaurants and bars, hotels and inns, tour companies and guides, all increased their focus on Savannah's rich history, recognizing this aspect of the city's appeal to tourists. In addition to the numerous house museums and specialized museums, it became common for commercial enterprises that were located in historic buildings to give emphasis to both factual and legendary aspects of the structures' nineteenth-century or early twentieth-century histories.

With the increasing recognition of the richness of the African American heritage, several sites documenting black history and achievements were erected or preserved and opened for visit in this period including some already mentioned.

In the year 2000, the Savannah Convention Center opened, across the river from the city front. Soon the center established four free ferries to visit the center on multiple

Savannah Irish and the St. Patrick's Day Parade

The annual Savannah St. Patrick's Day Parade is one of the largest and most recognized in the world. The first public observance of St. Patrick's Day with a parade in Savannah was in 1824, although there are records of private Irish parades prior to that date. The Savannah Hibernian Society traces its origins to 1812.

Before 1840, Irish immigrants to Savannah came mostly from Ulster—the "Scotch Irish," Protestant section now known as Northern Ireland. By 1850, it is estimated that 20 percent of Savannah citizens were Irish born. In the 1850s, some 80 percent of the Irish immigrants came from the Catholic counties of Ireland, and by 1876 the clear majority of Irish-born citizens of Savannah were Catholic.

Some of the groups that march in the modern St. Patrick's Day Parade can trace the roots of their organization well back into the nineteenth century. For example, the "Irish Jasper Greens," named for the Revolutionary hero William Jasper, was formed in 1842, and a unit of that group has marched in every St. Patrick's Day Parade in Savannah since that time. Another Irish organization, formed in 1876, was the Robert Emmet Association, named in honor of Robert Emmet, who led an unsuccessful revolt against British rule in 1803. That association was responsible for the naming of Emmet Park in 1903. The park had been previously known as the Strand or "Irish Green" for the number of nearby Irish residents.

Juliette Gordon Low Ferry. One of four Savannah Belles Ferries named after historical Savannah women, the *Juliette Gordon Low* regularly carries visitors along the riverfront and across to the Convention Center.

runs through the day from two stops on the city waterfront. The ferries were restored and reconfigured tugboats, each named for a historical woman, who, not incidentally, represented the elite white leadership of the city (*Juliette Gordon Low*), the white working class (*Florence Martus*), the African American heritage (*Susie King Taylor*), and the Native American heritage (*Mary Musgrove*).

Large new hotels supplanted the accommodations for visitors, while a number of smaller hotels and bed-and-breakfast inns in the Historic District opened in restored buildings. Construction and renovation of such properties continued from the 1990s through the present.

Along River Street, nearly every former warehouse was converted to house a business that welcomed the flow of tourists, with shops, restaurants, and hotels ranging from inexpensive to luxurious. River Street Market Place, about one block west of the Waving Girl Statue, first opened in 2003; it is an open-air market, with more than fifty stalls selling (mostly) inexpensive souvenir goods. A replica river steamboat, the *Georgia Queen*, offers dinner cruises, loading at 9 East River Street. The phone number for reservations on the steamboat is (912) 232-6404. These are only a few of the literally hundreds of ways in which enterprises have reflected the historic legacy of the city.

Georgia Queen. The *Georgia Queen* offers dinner cruises of the nearby Savannah River and docks on River Street just east of the Hyatt Regency Hotel and City Hall.

SITES

THE RALPH MARK GILBERT CIVIL RIGHTS MUSEUM (OPENED 1996, PERIOD OF FOCUS 1942–1960s)

460 Martin Luther King, Jr. Boulevard
(912) 777-6099

This museum is located in a rather modern building, in contrast to many of Savannah's historic sites. Built in 1914, it originally housed the Wage Earners' Savings and Loan Bank, established by Robert Pharrow. Pharrow was an African American contractor based in Atlanta, and the bank soon became known as the largest bank serving the black community in the United States. The bank building is on Martin Luther King, Jr. Boulevard, known at the time as West Broad Street; West Broad was the center of black-owned and black-operated businesses.

The museum is dedicated to documenting the history of the civil rights movement in Savannah, with a focus on the achievements of Ralph Mark Gilbert. Gilbert, the pastor of the First African Baptist Church on Franklin Square from 1939 to 1956, became head of the local chapter of the National Association for the Advancement of Colored People (NAACP) in 1942, serving until 1950. Under his leadership, the organization grew, and numerous chapters were established throughout Georgia.

Ralph Mark Gilbert Civil Rights Museum. This museum focuses on the civil rights movement in Savannah from the 1940s through the 1960s.

THE MERCER-WILLIAMS HOUSE (RESTORATION 1970s; SCANDAL 1981; NOVEL 1994; MOVIE 1997)

(912) 236-6352 (for tour reservations)

This house, facing Monterey Square on the western side of the square, at 429 Bull Street, was designed and begun in 1860 by New York architect John S. Norris for General Hugh Mercer, the great-grandfather of twentieth-century songwriter Johnny Mercer. The work on the house was interrupted by the Civil War and finished in 1868. However, members of the Mercer family never occupied the house.

In 1969, the home, which had fallen into disrepair, was purchased by Jim Williams, who had already earned a reputation for buying, restoring, and reselling older homes in Savannah. Altogether, Williams restored and sold about sixty historic homes in Savannah. After finishing the restoration of the Mercer House to its nineteenth-century elegance as a personal residence and office, Williams operated a thriving antiques restoration shop in the rear quarters of the building.

On May 2, 1981, in a dispute, Williams shot and killed his assistant, Danny Hansford, in his office in the home. After four trials, charges against Williams were dropped. Williams died of heart failure in 1990. The episodes of the death of Hansford and the trials of Jim Williams formed key parts of the fact-based novel by John Berendt, *Midnight in the Garden of Good and Evil*, published in 1994. The novel had an extraordinary run as a best seller, and a film by the same name, directed by Clint Eastwood, was released in 1997.

The publicity from the book and film brought increased national (and international) attention to several aspects of Savannah. Berendt's tale evoked the city's historical charm and

Mercer House. Made famous in the novel by John Berendt, *Midnight in the Garden of Good and Evil*, the Mercer House displays a fine collection of early nineteenth-century furnishings and artifacts.

preservation of buildings, its acceptance of the gay community, its preservation of black and white social elites and their institutions, and its reputation for supernatural encounters.

The movie version of the novel was set entirely in Savannah, and many scenes were filmed there. With its focus on unique cultural elements of the city, the movie probably stimulated tourism to the city more than all of the other movies set partially or entirely in Savannah.

Today the Mercer-Williams House is operated as a house museum by the sister of Jim Williams, Dorothy Kingery, a former professor at Armstrong Atlanta University. She remains active in Savannah historic preservation organizations. The focus of the tour of the Mercer-Williams House is on the nineteenth-century origins of the house and its furnishings. The ornate decor on display includes antique furniture, Chinese porcelain, and paintings from the 1700s and 1800s.

Movies Including Scenes Shot in Savannah

Film Title	Starring	Year Released
The Longest Yard	Burt Reynolds	1974
The Ordeal of Dr. Mudd	Dennis Weaver	1980
Glory	Denzel Washington	1989
Cape Fear	Robert De Niro	1991
Camilla	Jessica Tandy	1994
Forrest Gump	Tom Hanks	1994
Now and Then	Demi Moore	1994
Something to Talk About	Julia Roberts	1995
Midnight in the Garden of Good and Evil	Kevin Spacey	1997
The General's Daughter	John Travolta	1999
The Last Song	Miley Cyrus	2010
The Conspirator	Robin Wright	2010
Twelve Years a Slave	Chiwetel Ejiofor	2013

The two best-remembered films with Savannah scenes—of all the films on this list—are Forrest Gump *and* Midnight in the Garden of Good and Evil. *Major artifacts from each of these two films had to be removed from their original sites to protect them from souvenir hunters. The bench from* Forrest Gump *is now in the Savannah History Museum; the Bird Girl Statue from* Midnight in the Garden of Good and Evil *is in the Jepson Center.*

Forrest Gump. This replica of Forrest Gump sitting on a bench in Chippewa Park is found in the Georgia Tourist Information Center on Interstate 95, southbound, just south of the Georgia–South Carolina border. The original movie-prop bench is now in the Savannah History Museum.

CLUB ONE

1 Jefferson Street
(912) 232-0200

This nightclub offers a range of shows, including an impressive group of female impersonators. Catering to the LGBT community, the club received national publicity when it was described in John Berendt's *Midnight in the Garden of Good and Evil.* Berendt presented an engaging character description of "Lady Chablis," a performer at the club. She passed away in 2016.

Club One. Given international publicity with Berendt's novel and film, Club One still features risqué nightclub performances.

SAVANNAH COLLEGE OF ART AND DESIGN (SCAD) (1978–PRESENT)

Visitors to Savannah quickly realize that the city houses a unique college, with many separate buildings scattered throughout the Historic District and nearby communities. Within the city itself there are more than twenty instructional halls, each with separate specialties in art, design, and related disciplines, in addition to numerous administrative buildings and guest facilities. The unique citywide "campus" means that visitors to the Historic District encounter groups of SCAD students every few blocks, hurrying from one class to another, often carrying large portfolios of their current work. Some five thousand students are enrolled in the Savannah programs of the college, the largest art college in the United States.

The college was founded in 1978 by Richard Rowan, Paula Wallace, and May and Paul Poetter. The Poetters were the parents of Paula Wallace. Their objective was to provide college degree programs in art not available in this section of Georgia and to attract students from throughout the United States and from overseas. The first building acquired by the college was the Savannah Voluntary Guard Armory, now known as "Poetter Hall," on the corner of West Charlton Street and Bull Street, facing Madison Square. The building houses the admissions and "welcome" facilities, as well as a shop selling works produced by SCAD faculty and students.

One of the secrets of success of the college has been its practice of acquiring older buildings in Savannah and restoring and renovating them as instructional, administrative, or residential facilities. This method of expansion has won the college local support from the historic preservation community.

Poetter Hall. The first of many buildings restored and reused by Savannah College of Art and Design, Poetter Hall now offers art for sale as well as housing college administration offices.

Although still known as a college, the institution offers several graduate degree programs as well as bachelor degree programs. Accredited graduate degrees include master of architecture, master of arts, master of fine arts, and master of urban design. The college specializes in small classes and works closely with international students from some one hundred countries. In recent years, the college has opened other facilities in Atlanta and Vermont and abroad in Hong Kong, Great Britain, and the South of France.

SCAD has had many impacts on the community, some beyond the restoration of the numerous campus buildings scattered through the downtown. One is the neighborhood of remodeled and restored homes in the "Starland District."

THE STARLAND DISTRICT (1998–PRESENT)

This unofficial district of Savannah is south of Forsyth Park. It is a neighborhood roughly defined as a few blocks east and west of Bull Street, beginning about Thirty-Seventh Street and continuing south to about Victory Drive.

The name of the district comes from the Starland Dairy that opened about 1909, formed as a marketing cooperative for a number of dairy farmers in the Pooler area. The dairy occupied the whole block along Bull Street between Fortieth and Forty-First Streets. With a fleet of horse-drawn milk delivery wagons that were used into the 1950s, the business thrived, delivering returnable glass bottles of milk to customers' doorsteps. The recycled glass bottles are now collectors' items. However, by the 1980s, consumers had become used to purchasing milk at grocery and convenience stores. The Starland Dairy business fell on hard times and closed.

In 1998, two enterprising graduates of Savannah College of Art and Design, John Deaderick and Greg Jacobs, set out to apply their degrees in historic preservation, using the dairy building as a starting point. Their plan was to redevelop the dairy factory itself and to work on creating an "art and design district" centered around the building.

Within a few years, local artists had painted murals and graffiti on abandoned buildings. The interior courtyard of the dairy was decorated and served as a setting for art

Starlandia. One of several buildings representing the Starland District art neighborhood revival, this art supply store is at the center of the district.

shows and performances. The northern part of the dairy site itself developed into retail shops, studios, offices, and apartments, although most of the original factory was not redeveloped.

Meanwhile, the idea of an "arts district" did begin to attract new small businesses to the neighborhood. Some that succeeded later moved north of Forsyth Park into the central Historic District, but a few remained, helping to shape the neighborhood into its intended ambience of innovation, art, and alternative lifestyle. A visit to the neighborhood and especially the block between Fortieth and Forty-First Streets on Bull Street, the location of the original Starland Dairy and the heart of the district, gives a sense of the new ambience that Deaderick and Jacobs sought to establish. The distinctive red star of the dairy has become a symbol of the district.

OLYMPIC YACHTING CAULDRON MONUMENT (1996)

In 1996, the Olympic Games were held in Atlanta, Georgia. The 1996 games represented the hundredth anniversary of the first modern Olympics, and the Olympic Committee chose Atlanta over Athens, Greece, and other cities.

Since Atlanta is an inland city, Savannah was chosen as the headquarters site for the associated yachting events of the Olympics. This monument on the waterfront in Morrell Park, at the east end of River Street, is in memory of those events.

The monument was designed by Ivan Bailey, a Georgia sculptor. The monument is held up by five columns, representing the five Olympic rings, while six sails and copper flames capture the essence of the Olympic yachting events. The Olympic flame itself was landed in Savannah, and more than one hundred

Olympic Yachting Cauldron. This monument was erected in honor of the 1996 Olympics yachting events that were headquartered in Savannah.

thousand people turned out to watch it being carried through the city on its way to Atlanta. The yachting events took place July 20–29, 1996, in Wassaw Sound, some twenty miles east of Savannah, just south of Tybee Island, while the closing ceremonies for the yachting events were held in Savannah on August 2, 1996, two days before the official closing ceremonies for the Olympic events in Atlanta.

PIN POINT HERITAGE MUSEUM (FOCUS 1926–1985; OPENED 2012)

9924 Pin Point Avenue
(912) 355-0064

This museum, opened in 2012, documents the history of the small community of Pin

Oyster Factory, Pin Point. This museum in a former oyster factory is dedicated to the history of the small African American community found along the Moon River south of downtown Savannah.

Point, an Afro-American community with deep roots in Savannah history. The community was established in 1896, by Gullah/Geechee-speaking settlers who moved there from Ossabaw, Green, and Skidaway Islands, where a hurricane had devastated their homes.

The community soon opened a new church, the Sweetfield of Eden Baptist Church, in 1897. That church was also used as the town's school until 1926, when a school built by the Rosenwald Fund was opened. Julius Rosenwald, president of Sears Roebuck, worked with Booker T. Washington in establishing some five thousand schools for black children across the South.

The town thrived on several seafood operations, including shrimping, crabbing, and oyster harvesting and canning. Ben Bond and John Anderson Seafood opened in 1900. The Pin Point Heritage Museum itself is in a small

canning factory that had opened in 1926, processing oysters and crabs. That factory was set up by A. S. Varn.

The museum is on the shore of the Moon River, a marshy tidal waterway immortalized by Johnny Mercer in song. The factory provided employment to several generations of Pin Point residents for almost sixty years, closing in 1985.

Clarence Thomas was born in Pin Point in 1948; as a child, his first language was Gullah. He went on to attend Holy Cross College, located in Worcester, Massachusetts, and then Yale Law School. In 1990, President George H. W. Bush appointed Thomas to the United States Supreme Court, the second African American justice to serve there, following Thurgood Marshall. He spoke at the Sweetfield of Eden Baptist Church on the opening of the Pin Point Museum in 2012.

Pin Point mural. This mural documents the life and work of the Pin Point Gullah-Geechee community.

The Pin Point Heritage Museum exhibits start with a half-hour film and include historic photographs of the Varn factory and workers. Other exhibits include local art and artifacts, a striking exterior wall mural, information about the Gullah-Geechee heritage, and recordings of accounts of the work in the local seafood industry. Scheduled events include craft demonstrations.

Appendix A: African American History Sites and Tours

Note that many sites reflecting elements of African American heritage are mentioned in the main text and can be visited individually without using one of the organized tours. The churches and museums with a special focus on African American heritage are:

Beach Institute, 502 East Harris Street, (912) 234-8000

First African Baptist Church, 23 Montgomery Street, (912) 233-6597

First Bryan Baptist Church, 575 Bryan Street, (912) 232-5526

King-Tisdell Cottage, 514 East Huntingdon Street, (912) 234-8000

Pin Point Museum, 9924 Pin Point Avenue, (912) 355-0064

Ralph Mark Gilbert Civil Rights Museum, 460 Martin Luther King, Jr. Boulevard, (912) 777-6099

Several tours specialize in African American heritage sites and are listed below. Call for schedules, details of sites visited, costs, and reservations:

First African Baptist Church, (912) 233-6597

Follow the Drinking Gourd, (912) 257-7255

Footprints of Savannah, (912) 695-3872

Gullah Geechee Talkin' Tour, (912) 721-8778

Houses of Praise, (912) 721-8778

The Indigo Journey Walking Tour, (912) 224-0973

"Jubilee Is Here": The Abolitionist Movement, (912) 721-8778

Slaves in the City, (912) 721-8778

Appendix B: Ghost Sites and Tours

Savannah is famous for its ghost stories and ghost tours. Among the individual sites commonly visited as locations for paranormal episodes by local guides are the following:

Sorrell-Weed House, 6 West Harris Street. Reputedly the "most haunted" house in Savannah and the "fifth most haunted" in the United States.

Andrew Low House, 329 Abercorn Street. Stories include sightings of the ghost of Robert E. Lee; Tom, a onetime butler in the home; and Juliette Gordon Low herself.

17Hundred90 Inn, 307 East President Street. Many ghost tours include a stop here. The ghost of "Anne" is associated with room 204, where she supposedly committed suicide by jumping to her death. Researchers dispute the historical accuracy of the accounts.

Mercer-Williams House, 429 Bull Street. Stories include one involving a child, Tommy Downs, who fell from the roof in 1969 while chasing pigeons and was impaled on the iron fence.

The Pirates' House Restaurant, 20 East Broad Street. Sightings include odd phenomena in various locations, including the underground rooms.

The Marshall House, 123 East Broughton Street. Still an active hotel, encounters and paranormal phenomena include sink faucets that turn on and off by themselves, flickering lights, and unexplained voices in the hallways. There have been reports of doorknobs inexplicably wiggling and crashing noises in the early morning hours.

The Gribble House, 234 Martin Luther King, Jr. Boulevard. A triple murder in 1909 has spawned several stories and legends.

Moon River Brewing Company, 21 West Bay Street. Built in 1821, the old structure has led to several tales, including one involving "Toby," who hangs out in the bar's billiard room, sometimes pushing or bumping customers. Some visitors report an unexplained severe chill while touring the building's basement.

Olde Pink House Restaurant, 23 Abercorn Street. Visitors report the appearance of its creator, James Habersham Jr., who has been supposedly sighted in colonial-era outfits, drinking ale.

Cemeteries. Each cemetery has several ghost legends associated with it.

Colonial Park Cemetery, at Abercorn and Oglethorpe Streets. Burials in this cemetery stopped in 1855, and many of the graves are unmarked.

Bonaventure Cemetery, out of town a few miles by way of Skidaway Road and Thirty-Sixth Street, is described in chapter 5; it has a well-earned reputation as picturesque.

TOURS

Each ghost or paranormal tour is slightly different, and serious or casual paranormal tourists should compare rates, reputations, and tour details and sites to be visited, as some tours have better online reviews than others and each includes a different set of locations. Companies offering tours in 2018 included the following, although this is not a complete list of all such tours:

Blue Orb Savannah Ghost Tours, (912) 665-4258

Haunted Savannah Tours, (912) 445-5027

Ghost City Tours/Grave Tales, (888) 859-5375

Ghosts and Gravestones, (912) 226-6782

Hearse Ghost Tours, (912) 695-1578

The Savannah Ghostwalker Tour, (912) 662-0155

Savannah Ghost Walks and Events, (912) 508-1234

Sixth Sense World, (912) 292-0960

Appendix C: Museums and House Museums

Some of the following museums and house museums are also discussed in the text. This list is provided so that visitors can directly check hours and rates, which are subject to change.

MUSEUMS

Beach Institute, 502 East Harris, (912) 335-8868
Georgia State Railroad Museum, 665 Louisville Road, (912) 651-6823
Massie Heritage Museum, 207 East Gordon, (912) 395-5070
Mighty Eighth Air Force Museum, 175 Bourne Avenue, Pooler, GA, (912) 748-8888
Pin Point Heritage Museum, 9924 Pin Point Avenue, (912) 355-0064
Prohibition Museum, 209 West Julian Street, (912) 220-1249
Ralph Mark Gilbert Civil Rights Museum, 460 MLK Boulevard, (912) 777-6099
Savannah History Museum, 303 MLK Boulevard, (912) 651-6825
SCAD Museum of Art, 601 Turner Boulevard, (912) 525-7191
Ships of the Sea Museum, 41 MLK Boulevard, (912) 232-1511
Telfair Museums, 207 West York Street, (912) 790-8800
Telfair Academy, 121 Barnard Street, (912) 790-8800
Jepson Center, 207 West York Street, (912) 790-8800
Owens-Thomas House, 124 Abercorn Street, (912) 790-8800
Webb Military Museum, 411 East York, (912) 663-0398

HOUSE MUSEUMS

Davenport, 324 East State Street, (912) 236-8097
Flannery O'Connor, 207 East Charlton, (912) 233-6014
Green-Meldrim, 14 West Macon, (912) 233-3845
Harper-Fowlkes, 230 Barnard, (912) 234-2180
Juliette Gordon Low, 10 East Oglethorpe, (912) 233-4501
Mercer-Williams, 429 Bull, (912) 236-6352
Sorrell-Weed, 6 West Harris, (912) 257-2223

Bibliographic Note

This book is part of a series originally published by Pineapple Press of Sarasota, Florida. The series includes:

St. Augustine in History, 2014

Key West in History, 2015

Charleston in History, 2016

Tampa Bay in History, 2017

In all of these works, Loretta Carlisle provides the photographs, supplemented with a few historical images derived from archival sources. Rodney Carlisle researches and writes the text, edited by Loretta and Pineapple Press editors.

Loretta Carlisle brings her experience in providing photographs to illustrate a number of prior books, including *Handbook to Life in America* (a nine-volume series, 2009); *One Day in History: July 4, 1776* (2006); *One Day in History: December 7, 1941* (2006); and *The Forts of Florida* (2012).

The approach of the books we have produced on St. Augustine, Key West, Charleston, Tampa, and Savannah is based on a "public history" orientation. That viewpoint was pioneered by writers like David Kyvig and Myron A. Marty, whose book *Nearby History: Exploring the Past around You* was originally published in 1982 and is still in print in an updated edition, published by Rowman & Littlefield. Kyvig and Marty focus on history as viewed and documented by three-dimensional objects, rather than paper in the form of books, letters, newspapers, and official documents as conventionally used as sources.

"Public history," as the term is professionally employed, refers to the study, preservation, presentation, and production of historical materials outside of academia. Public history refers to work in archives, in museums, for corporations and other institutions, and in governmental agencies. In each of these public history settings, researchers are concerned with preserving and presenting history, not simply for access by students and academics but also to bring it to wider audiences. It is with that orientation that this series of guides to the three-dimensional "documents" in these historic cities of Florida, South Carolina, and Georgia are presented.

In researching this volume, in addition to visiting the sites and collections in Savannah and gathering local information in the form of local guidebooks, brochures, and historical markers, the authors made use of several specific published books and internet sources. Those included:

Busch, John Laurence. *Steam Coffin: Captain Moses Rogers and the Steamship Savannah Break the Barrier.* Chicago: Hodos Historia, 2010.

Daiss, Timothy. *Rebels, Saints, and Sinners: Savannah's Rich and Colorful Personalities.* Gretna, LA: Pelican, 2002.

Freeman, Ron. *Savannah: People, Places and Events.* Savannah, GA: Published by the author, 1997.

Rauers, Betty Wannamaker, and Franklin S. Traub. *Sojourn in Savannah. 8th ed.* Savannah, GA: City of Savannah, 1990.

Russell, Preston, and Barbara Hines. *Savannah: A History of Her People since 1733.* Savannah, GA: Frederic C. Beil, 1992.

Savannah Morning News. *Our Savannah: Your Free Insider's Guide to the Hostess City of the South* Savannah, GA: Savannah Morning News, 2018.

Wilkes, Sema. *Mrs. Wilkes' Boarding House Cookbook.* Berkeley, CA: Ten Speed, 2001.

Among the most useful, well-researched, and reliable items that we found on the internet were the following:

The New Georgia Encyclopedia (https://www.georgiaencyclopedia.org/)

Visit Historic Savannah (http://www.visit-historic-savannah.com/)

In addition, we consulted a variety of scholarly articles on individuals and special topics related to Savannah history found through JSTOR, the online repository of articles published in professional journals.

Index

About the Authors

Rodney Carlisle is professor emeritus of history at Rutgers University and the author of more than forty books. **Loretta Carlisle** is a professional photographer. They live in Carlisle, Pennsylvania, and the Villages, Florida.